HOW TO
RECOGNIZE
& REWARD
EMPLOYEES

The WorkSmart Series

CONTENTS

PART III. 100 WAYS TO RECOGNIZE & REWARD PEOPLE

PREFACE

Every time employees are surveyed about what they want most from their jobs, recognition for work well done ranks high among their responses. Employees who get that recognition tend to have higher self-esteem, more confidence, more willingness to take on new challenges, and more eagerness to contribute new ideas and improve productivity.

There is clear evidence that more and more organizations are getting the message that recognizing employees is good for business. "Employee of the Month" photos look down at us from the walls of supermarkets and from behind the cashiers in restaurants. They gaze at us as we check into hotels and even smile out from corridor walls in hospitals.

What's less clear is the extent to which the practice of recognizing and rewarding employees regularly for their day-to-day accomplishments has permeated all levels of the organization. While the workplace wall sports a new picture each month, many employees are still saying, "The only time my manager notices my work is when I do something wrong" or "Nobody ever says 'thank you' around here" or even "Our manager takes the credit for all our successes."

Good managers recognize people by doing things that acknowledge their accomplishments. They reward people by giving them something tangible, but not necessarily costly, in return for their efforts. And they create environments where jobs provide intrinsic rewards—good feelings people get from doing the work itself. Yet in too many organizations, recognition is reserved for an elite few and rewards are defined solely in terms of wages and salaries. This book is about what managers at all levels can do to recognize and reward more employees, more often, and more effectively to improve morale, productivity, and work quality.

The book is divided into three parts, which answer the questions why, how, and what? Why recognize and reward employees? To some the answer is self-evident, but to others the need to provide employees with anything beyond a paycheck is still in question. Part I offers three reasons: equity, motivation, and clarification of what is important to the organization.

Part II is about how to recognize and reward employees in order to increase their motivation to engage in behaviors and produce outcomes that contribute to achieving the goals of the organization. It contains ten guidelines for developing and implementing both formal recognition and reward programs and informal behaviors that provide spontaneous recognition to deserving employees.

Part III suggests 100 specific ways you can recognize and reward people in your organization. Out of the 100 offered here, you will surely find some that are appropriate for your organization or that trigger new ideas of your own for the best ways to acknowledge the contributions of those who report to you.

PART

THREE REASONS TO RECOGNIZE & REWARD EMPLOYEES

By recognizing and rewarding employees, management:

- Establishes an equity arrangement, providing employees with a fair return for their efforts.
- Motivates them to maintain and improve their performance.
- Clarifies what behaviors and outcomes the company values.

EQUITY:

A FAIR DAY'S WORK FOR A FAIR DAY'S . . . WHAT?

All organizations acknowledge the need to establish an equitable balance between the employee's contribution to the organization and of the organization's contribution to the employee. Meeting that need is the first reason to recognize and reward employees. But just what reward balances the proverbial fair day's work?

A fair day's pay? Certainly, that is the first thing that comes to mind. But many managers feel they have little control over the paychecks of the people who work for them. Locked into an organizationwide compensation system, they are often frustrated by the narrow latitude they have for adjusting wages and salaries to fit each employee's hopes and expectations. Even first-line managers do, however, have a significant role to play in balancing work and pay. We will explore this role later in this chapter.

Just as important is the realization that pay is not the only thing people work for. They are looking for a number of other returns to justify the time, energy, and mental and emotional effort they devote to the organization. Equity requires that the organization contribute to meeting employees' needs for esteem, creative challenge, professional growth, and socialization to the same degree that employees contribute to meeting the objectives of the organization. In exchange for helping the manager reach the goals of the work unit, employees have every right to expect the manager to help them meet their goals.

THREE EQUITY EQUATIONS

All of this can be summed up in Equity Equation 1:

> What the employee receives from the employer must be equal in value to the quality and quantity of work done by the employee.

For employees to verify Equity Equation 1, they must have a way to determine the worth of their work. To some degree they do this by gut feel, but they validate their feelings by making two comparisons. They compare what they receive from their employer with what other people in the organization receive for doing similar work, They also compare what they receive with what is received by people doing similar work in other organizations. These comparisons give rise to two more equity equations.

Equity Equation 2 is:

> What the employee receives from the employer must be equal in value to what is received by other employees doing similar work of similar quality and quantity.

Equity Equation 3 is:

> What the employee receives from the employer must be equal in value to what is received by people who do similar work for other organizations.

In making these two comparisons, the first thing employees will weigh is paychecks, but as they balance the equations for themselves they will factor in their opportunities to do interesting and challenging work, the recognition they receive for their accomplishments, even the ambience of their working environment. A single work unit or an entire company in which these rewards are clearly superior will retain loyal, high-performing employees even if the financial

What rewards do employees value most? Praise and freedom, say two CEOs.

rewards are lower there than in other units or other organizations.

When asked what rewards employees value most in their companies, the CEOs of several mid-size to large corporations give a number of responses that don't involve money at all. "Praise is as important as tangible rewards," states the president of a growing company in the home health care field in Cincinnati. Employees there set monthly goals and are recognized for reaching them at meetings between managers and employees called accountability sessions. The head of another home health care company, based in Georgia but with offices in twenty states, has found that the reward his people appreciate most is the freedom to do their jobs as they think best.

SELF-EXAMINATION
UNDERSTANDING THE MANAGER'S ROLE IN MAINTAINING EQUITY

Take this brief true/false quiz to examine your own expectations of what a manager can do to balance the value of an employee's work, on the one hand, against the value of what that employee receives in return from the organization.

1. If the people who report to me feel they are not being fairly rewarded, there is nothing I can do about it. It's the fault of the organization's compensation system.   T   F

2. The only way to get employees to do more or better work is to pay them more.   T   F

3. When times are tough, just having a job is reward enough for many employees.   T   F

4. Some of the people who report to me have a very inflated idea of their own

worth. They expect above-average raises
for pretty mediocre performance.   T   F

5. What other employees make is no
business of anyone who reports to me,
and people have no right to compare their
salaries to anyone else's.   T   F

6. I'm tired of hearing that other companies
pay better than this one. If my employees
think some other company is so great,
let them get jobs there.   T   F

7. The best way to make pay equitable
among the people who work for me is to
pay them all about the same.   T   F

8. If people who report to me complain that
employees in other parts of the company
earn more than they do, I point out that
I'm in the same boat, making less than
many other managers do.   T   F

9. If I can't give an employee the raise I think
she deserves, I promise to make it up to
her next year.   T   F

10. The happiest employees are those who
make the most money.   T   F

Scoring

If you answered True to any of the questions in the preceding
quiz, the goal of this book is to change your mind and to
provide you with new ideas and techniques for dealing with
the problems involved. Many of the issues are covered in
more depth in this and succeeding chapters, but a quick
analysis follows.

1. **False.** By the way they communicate and apply the
compensation system, managers can influence employees'
perceptions of its fairness. Equally important is to recognize

that salary is only one of several rewards that go into the equity equations. Managers can create an environment that boosts employees' self-esteem, provides opportunities for creativity and growth, and allows them to enjoy the rewards that are inherent in interesting and challenging work.

2. **False.** Actually, increased pay quickly becomes an entitlement rather than an incentive to work harder. Recognition and the more intrinsic rewards noted in the analysis of question 1 are often more effective in the long run.

3. **False.** Just having a job may be reward enough to keep people coming to work in tough times, but fear of losing it tends to encourage employees to retract into safe, conventional behavior and to avoid innovation and risk taking.

4. **False.** Managers should ensure that their employees know, for each of their tasks, what represents unsatisfactory, average, and above-average performance and what kind of compensation they can expect for each.

5. **False.** Whether employees *should* know what other people earn is irrelevant. They *do* find out, because it is one factor that feeds into their equity equations. Managers who ignore employee resentment about perceived inequities should expect that resentment to build and affect performance.

6. **False.** Managers with this attitude lose their best workers and retain only those not good enough to get better-paying jobs elsewhere. On the other hand, good workers will often stay with an organization that pays less than its competitors do if the total reward package (see the analysis of question 1) is favorable and distributed fairly within the organization.

7. **False.** Paying everyone the same encourages mediocre performance from everyone and builds resentment among the best performers.

8. **False.** Sharing your salary dissatisfactions with your employees undermines your credibility and their sense of satisfaction in working for you. Instead of sanctioning their

dissatisfaction, focus on building a work environment that makes working for your unit its own reward.

9. **False.** Despite your best intentions, too much can happen in a year that may undermine your ability to fulfill your promise. If you don't, the affected employee will become doubly embittered.

10. **False.** The happiest employees are those who enjoy doing their work and who are recognized for their accomplishments.

BUT WHAT ABOUT MONEY?

Certainly money is the most obvious component in the equity equations, so its importance as a reward can't be dismissed. Even if you don't set compensation policy, there is much you can do to influence how it is perceived by the people who report to you.

Managers can influence how employees perceive the equity of their income and their raises by:

• *Developing a thorough understanding of the organization's financial picture and of how the salary budget fits into that picture.* Even many managers fall into the trap of bemoaning an austere salary budget rather than familiarizing themselves with the financial realities behind it and learning what impact the salary budget is expected to have on the organization's financial results.

• *Communicating the facts of the salary budget, the financial bottom line, and the organization's long-term expectations clearly, completely, and objectively.* This kind of communication serves two purposes. First, it is a form of employee recognition, since it acknowledges that employees are intelligent enough to understand, valuable enough to be informed, and trustworthy enough to be included. Second, it inserts a new variable into the equity equations: How much can the organization afford? Otherwise satisfied employees will qualify their definition of a fair day's pay to reflect their understanding of what the organization can afford under the current circumstances.

• *Rewarding above-average performance evaluations with above-average pay increases.* The perception of equity breaks down when employees whose performance is rated "excellent" or "exceptional" get pay raises that only match the salary increase average. This is a problem in work units where all or most of the employees are highly regarded workers who have regularly been rated very highly. Without some poor performers to balance the high ones, managers find it difficult to give above-average raises to everyone and stay within their budgets. Some managers appeal successfully to upper management for a bigger share of the pie. Otherwise, it may be time to rethink the meaning of *average*. Logically, if everyone is performing above-average, the perception of average is too low. Some managers may need to raise the bar at the beginning of a performance cycle and let employees know early on that they must meet some very specific challenges in order to earn a higher rating and a higher raise.

A CHECKLIST FOR APPLYING THE PRINCIPLES OF EQUITY

In the perception of those who report to you, which equity equations need balancing in your work unit?

☐ Reward equals work.

☐ Employees receive comparable rewards for comparable work.

☐ Rewards in the organization are comparable to rewards in other organizations.

What can you do to begin to balance the equity equations in the perception of your employees? Check all that apply.

☐ Gain a better understanding of the company's financial situation and the impact of the salary budget and compensation system on that situation, short- and long-term.

☐ Communicate to employees the facts about the salary budget, placing it in the context of the organization's financial picture and short- and long-term expectations.

☐ At the beginning of the salary year, or the start of the performance management cycle, ensure that each employee knows, for each part of the job, what represents unsatisfactory, average, and above-average performance.

☐ With employee input, redefine *average* and *above-average* performance to ensure that truly above-average performers earn above-average salary increases.

☐ Focus on meeting employee needs for esteem, creative challenge, professional growth, and socialization.

☐ Begin to build a work environment that makes working in your unit its own reward.

MOTIVATION:

INCENTIVES TO MAINTAIN AND IMPROVE PERFORMANCE

Purists insist that no one can motivate another person, that all motivation comes from within. So the best way to start this chapter is with a definition of terms. What this book means by *motivating* other people is inspiring individuals and teams to do the best possible job by creating an environment in which they want to perform to the best of their abilities. This definition recognizes that there are plenty of ways a manager can influence the strength of an employee's internal motivation.

One way is to provide incentives, in the form of recognition and rewards, to encourage people to maintain an excellent performance or improve an unsatisfactory performance. Invariably the first incentive that comes to mind is money, but for most managers, motivating with money confronts two obstacles. The first is their limited control over financial rewards for their employees. The second is that money's success as a motivator is erratic at best.

IS MONEY A MOTIVATOR?

As a motivator, money has three strikes against it:

1. *Its impact is short-lived.* Most major financial rewards come annually, and the effect wears off long before the year is out. A nice bonus or a big raise may inspire a spurt of activity from a grateful employee, but once the bonus is

spent or living expenses swell to meet the raise (as they always do), the reward and its motivational value become history.

2. *What starts out as a reward for exceptional performance tends to become perceived as an entitlement.* A bonus or an unusually large raise is special the first time, maybe even the second time, but after that the recipient comes to expect it as part of business as usual.

3. *When people are paid to do specific tasks, the money tends to supplant intrinsic motivation.* People often do extra work for the pure enjoyment of performing the task, the satisfaction of solving a problem, or the excitement of confronting a challenge. But when they know they will get a bonus or incentive compensation for performing this work, they will perceive themselves as doing it for the money rather than for the intrinsic, more sustaining motivation.

If money is so unsatisfactory a motivator, then why is it always an issue? As item 1 points out, its impact is short-lived. Companies that depend on it as their chief motivator can never give enough of it to keep people satisfied. But there are other reasons why the power of money cannot be discounted.

Money is how you keep score.

—H. Wayne Huizenga Chairman of Blockbuster Entertainment Corporation and said to be one of the richest men in America (quoted in *The New York Times Magazine*, Dec. 5, 1993)

For one thing, while the presence of money may not be a very good motivator, the absence of it is a strong demotivator. When financial rewards don't meet the equity equations discussed in the chapter on "Equity," need may force employees to go elsewhere, or resentment may induce lethargy or even sabotage.

Equally important, money is used as a scorecard. It's one way people measure achievement, their importance to the organization, and their standing among others in the organization as well as in the larger community.

But money needn't be the only way to keep score. Managers with little access to financial rewards for their employees can give points to their workers in a variety of other, often more motivating, ways. And many people are motivated by things that can't be measured at all.

IF NOT MONEY, THEN WHAT?

People are motivated to fulfill a number of different needs, the most basic being to get a roof over their heads and food in their mouths. The most lofty need perhaps is to transcend the mundane and reach the highest level of achievement and spirituality (what motivation theorist Abraham Maslow called self-actualization). But what drives people the strongest varies from one individual to another, and for any individual the need may change depending upon the situation. At any given time an individual may be driven primarily by the need for security, socialization, esteem, achievement, or power—or some combination of these.

The reward that an employee values most—and that provides the greatest incentive to maintain and improve performance—will be the one that contributes to the fulfillment of that person's strongest drives. The challenge for the manager is to recognize what each employee is seeking and to identify ways to reward the employee by satisfying that need.

EXERCISE 1
NONMONETARY REWARDS
THAT MOTIVATE

The columns below contain first, descriptions of employees, second, a list of possible driving needs, and third, a list of various rewards. For each employee, determine the most likely driving need and the two rewards that are most appropriate for fulfilling that need. (Use a reward only once even though some rewards may seem appropriate to fulfill more than one need. Try to select the best two for each need.)

Employee Description	Needs	Rewards

Employee Description

I. The employee has complained about feeling isolated and needing more interaction with others on the job.

    Probable need: _____

    Appropriate rewards:

    _____

    _____

II. A good worker who is helpful to others writes you memos documenting each of her accomplishments.

    Probable need: _____

    Appropriate rewards:

    _____

    _____

III. The employee constantly seeks new assignments and dedicates himself to solving problems and mastering challenges.

    Probable need: _____

    Appropriate rewards:

    _____

    _____

IV. Although the employee's job is not in serious danger, she has become nervous and withdrawn as the company has gone through a series of downsizings.

Needs

a. Security

b. Socializing

c. Esteem

d. Achievement

e. Power

Rewards

1. A letter of praise sent to the boss's boss and a copy of it given to the employee

2. The right to choose and manage a project

3. A department party

4. An opportunity to work on a project team

5. An opportunity to learn new skills that are greatly in demand in the organization

6. An opportunity to help develop an important new product for the company

7. Testimonials from peers attesting to their high regard for the employee

8. A team leadership assignment

9. Assurances that the employee's job is not in danger of being eliminated

10. An assignment to develop and implement a program that's never been used in the company before

Employee Description	Needs	Rewards
Probable need: _____		
Appropriate rewards:		
_____		
_____		

V. A high-performing employee who likes being in charge of projects is frustrated because the company is not promoting people into management positions.

Probable need: _____

Appropriate rewards:

_____

_____

Answers

I. *b.*, 3, 4; II. *c.*, 1, 7; III. *d.*, 6, 10; IV. *a.*, 5,9; V. *e.*, 2, 8.

MOTIVATING TOP PERFORMERS

There is no shortage of ways to recognize and reward high-performing employees. All the rewards listed in Exercise 1 are suitable, and throughout this book you'll find numerous more. Unfortunately, managers too often take for granted that their top performers are self-motivated, and forget to nurture that motivation until it's too late and performance slips or the employee finds another job.

The best thing about nonmonetary rewards is that they are always available. Use them as frequently as you can, being especially generous—but always sincere—with thank-you's, warm praise, and exposure to upper management.

Most important, be very specific about the behavior or outcome you are recognizing. A general "thanks for the good work" doesn't really convince someone that you've paid much attention to what she has been doing. You'll have a much stronger impact with something like this:

> Thanks for the energy and long hours you've dedicated to developing the new tracking system. What you've accomplished will save us all time and money. In fact, I've just used it and gotten my answer in half the time it used to take.

That statement illustrates some keys to effective praise. So, whenever possible:

1. Be specific about what you are praising.
2. Acknowledge both the effort and the outcome.
3. State the impact on the organization.
4. State the impact on you personally.

MOTIVATING POOR PERFORMERS

Using recognition and rewards to motivate poor performers presents an apparent paradox. Equity Equation 1 (see the chapter on "Equity") states that rewards must be equal to the quantity and quality of work done by the employee. Under this principle, high performers will receive much more recognition and many more rewards than will low performers. But it may be the low performers whom the manager most needs to motivate.

Catch them doing something right.

—KENNETH BLANCHARD AND SPENCER JOHNSON
The One Minute Manager

To motivate poor performers, you need to recognize small improvements and positive changes in processes and procedures, even if outcomes aren't yet up to par. Such incremental advances hardly warrant a bonus or a testimonial dinner, but they should be rewarded with an honest show of appreciation. One of the great characteristics of the phrase *Thank you* (more about it in Guideline 6) is that it's as appropriate for small accomplishments as for major ones.

Being specific is as important in motivating a poor performer as in recognizing a top performer—maybe even more so. Since your goal is for the employee to repeat and further improve on one satisfactory behavior among a host of unsatisfactory ones, you need to clarify very precisely what that satisfactory behavior is. Otherwise, you risk validating other behaviors you are hoping to change. Here's the kind of statement that reinforces a specific behavior:

> Thanks for the extra time you spent to finish the filing before you went to lunch. Because you did that, I was able to quickly find the letter from Jarvis when she called. That put me in a much better position to negotiate a better deal for us.

Notice that this statement contains all the keys to effective praise listed under "Motivating Top Performers." Yet it doesn't overbalance Equity Equation 1 by reacting out of proportion to the employee's behavior.

When you use recognition and rewards to motivate an employee, whether a fast tracker or an underachiever, your goal is to reinforce successful behaviors so that the employee will repeat them and apply the same dedication to other tasks.

CLARIFICATION:

WHAT'S REALLY IMPORTANT TO THE COMPANY?

What management rewards, more than all the mission and value statements ever written, tells employees what's really important to the company.

When promotions and plum assignments go to people who contribute new ideas and try new ways of doing things, workers get the message that the company means it when it professes to value innovation and risk taking. But leaders who proclaim the importance of taking risks might as well shout into the wind if they surround themselves with lieutenants whose only risk lies in tripping over their feet when they click their heels and say, "Yes, boss." When the company says one thing and rewards another, the troops know enough to take their cues from actions, not words.

So the third major function of recognizing and rewarding employees is clarifying what behaviors and outcomes the organization values most. Especially during a culture change, when people are unsure of what the organization expects, this function of recognition and rewards is very powerful.

SUPPORTING THE VALUES OF THE ORGANIZATION

In recent years, many organizations have codified sets of values, committed them to paper, and circulated them widely among employees, customers, and the outside community. Most statements include words and phrases like *customer satisfaction, honesty and integrity, innovation and risk taking, teamwork, good citizenship, employee development,* and *profitability.* These are not just abstract qualities. If they are meaningful, then they require certain behaviors.

You can support your organization's values by recognizing and rewarding those behaviors among the people who report to you. With the help of your employees, identify specific behaviors that demonstrate or uphold each value, then reward your employees for behaving in those ways. If your values statement lists honesty and integrity, then someone who admits to making a mistake deserves to be rewarded, not vilified. (That doesn't mean releasing the person from the responsibility for correcting the error.)

When your organization is in the midst of a culture change, some appropriate behaviors may be new and even threatening. Don't wait for a dramatic change to occur before recognizing their efforts to adapt. If two or three people informally join forces to get a task done in record time, for example, acknowledge publicly or with a token award that they are furthering the value of teamwork. By recognizing even small moves in the right direction, you can encourage people to go on making more major changes.

VALUES AND BEHAVIORS

To be meaningful, organization values need to be translated into behaviors. Below are some goals that turn up on most corporate values statements, along with examples of corresponding behaviors (mostly low-key, not monumental) that deserve recognition from you when your employees engage in them.

*Customer
satisfaction:*   • Staying calm when confronted by an irate
                       customer

(continues)

- Helping people in other departments (they're customers too)
- Providing a little more than the customer asks for

Honesty and integrity:

- Giving credit for a borrowed idea
- Correcting defects, even if others don't notice them
- Admitting to a mistake

Innovation and risk taking:

- Experimenting with a new process even if the old one's not "broke"
- Volunteering for a task the person has never done before
- Contributing new ideas

Teamwork:

- Pitching in and helping a coworker who is behind schedule
- Asking others to participate in a high-profile plum assignment
- Changing work habits, e.g., arrival time, to meet the team's needs

Good citizenship:

- Organizing a program to tutor schoolchildren
- Participating in school career nights
- Coaching a company-sponsored Little League team

Employee development:

- Learning a new system that will benefit the department
- Coaching a coworker
- Making a lateral career move to learn a new function

Profitability:

- Seeking competent, less costly vendors
- Recycling to reduce purchases
- Seeking new markets for existing products or services

EXERCISE 2
SUPPORTING YOUR
ORGANIZATION'S VALUES

Fill in the spaces below as follows:
1. List your organization's stated values.
2. List behaviors in your work unit that support each value.
    List the people who have demonstrated these behaviors (even in small ways) and deserve recognition.

Value: _____

   Behaviors: _____

                 _____

                 _____

   People: _____

                 _____

                 _____

Value: _____

   Behaviors: _____

                 _____

                 _____

   People: _____

                 _____

                 _____

Value: _____

   Behaviors: _____

                 _____

                 _____

People: _____

_____

_____

Value: _____

Behaviors: _____

_____

_____

People: _____

_____

_____

Value: _____

Behaviors: _____

_____

_____

People: _____

_____

_____

BUT DO THEY KNOW WHAT THE REWARD IS FOR?

Here's a quick quiz. Assume you are a manager anxious to support your company president's broadly stated plea for more risk taking. You champion an employee's plan to implement a significant new work process, but the new process is a failure, costing time and money and providing no measureable improvement in output. Still, wanting to continue to encourage risk-taking behavior, you reward the effort by giving this employee an opportunity to manage another innovative project. What will your other employees assume you are rewarding?

- Failure?
- Your favorite employee, no matter how the person screws up?
- Risk-taking behavior, which you have distinguished from outcome?

There is no sure answer, is there? Clearly, the reward in this type of situation has a high chance of being misunderstood. Therefore, you need to be very clear about your reasons for giving a reward, especially if it is for a behavior, not an outcome. You can lessen the probability of misunderstandings if you:

1. Make it clear at the outset that you want people to try out new behaviors, even when the outcomes are not sure bets.
2. Enlist your employees' input as you determine what behaviors deserve to be rewarded. If they have helped to identify them, they will be more likely to recognize these behaviors in the actions of their coworkers.
3. Distinguish between reasonable behavior that carries a risk and poor business practices.
4. Clarify the degree of risk (e.g., financial) that is tolerable.
5. Let people know that if they stay within the guidelines of reasonable behavior and tolerable risk, you will reward the behavior regardless of the outcome.
6. Be consistent in your treatment of all employees.

CREATING ROLE MODELS

When you publicly recognize and reward an employee, you hope to create a role model for the rest of the organization. But for others to follow the model's lead, they need to:

1. Understand specifically, in terms of behaviors and outcomes, what the person did to be singled out in this way.

2. Know how the role model's performance relates to their jobs.
3. Be confident that they will receive similar treatment if they make similar contributions.

To meet these three needs, you need to:

1. Describe the recognized behaviors and outcomes at a meeting of your staff. You might also distribute a written description.
2. Meet separately with each employee to jointly identify ways in which each person can apply parallel behavior to achieve similar outcomes. Help each employee set personal goals.
3. Earn employees' trust by being consistent over time in your treatment of everyone who reports to you.

PART

TEN GUIDELINES FOR RECOGNIZING & REWARDING EMPLOYEES

What gives a reward value in the eyes of employees? More than just its price tag. Some organizations get more mileage out of a handshake than others do with a big bonus. The difference is in how the rewards are administered. Your recognition and reward system will have more impact if you:

- Involve employees in designing the system.
- Determine and communicate specific reward criteria.
- Reward everyone who meets the criteria, not just a chosen few.
- Recognize behaviors as well as outcomes.
- Individualize rewards—give people what they want.
- Say "thank you" a lot.
- Make it your goal to boost workers' self-esteem and their esteem in the eyes of others.
- Develop an atmosphere that fosters intrinsic rewards.
- Reward the entire team for team accomplishments.
- Avoid deadly mistakes that cause your reward system to backfire.

GUIDELINE 1

DETERMINE YOUR GOALS AND GET EMPLOYEE INPUT

Check any statements below that you've heard in your workplace during the past year:

☐ "I don't know what you have to do to get any appreciation around here."

☐ "Why should I work harder just to get a dumb plaque (or certificate, paperweight, trophy)?"

☐ "Sure, the company gives out awards, but not for anything I do on my job."

☐ "If you get an award, everybody thinks you've been ingratiating yourself with the boss [probably expressed in a more colloquial way]."

☐ "The awards are rigged so that the same people get them every year."

☐ "If I tried to compete for that award, I'd never have time to get any other work done."

☐ "I'd have to clone myself and work twenty-four hours a day to meet the qualifications for an award."

☐ "You can do a great job here but still never get an award."

That's a host of common complaints, but you can minimize all of them, at least in connection with the rewards you control, with one strategy: Involve your employees in developing and administering your work unit's reward system. They, better than anyone else, know the tasks and requirements of their jobs. With their help, you can establish a reward system that not only fills their needs better than one you create alone but also has more credibility.

Revisiting the complaints, one at a time, let's look at the potential benefits of employee involvement. When employees have input into the reward system, they:

- Know what they have to do to earn a reward, because they've established the criteria.
- Value the reward more because they also value what it represents. Objects like plaques and trophies have no intrinsic worth, but displaying them is an acceptable way for an employee to tell the world, "I did a great job at a task I'm proud of, and my management and peers were impressed."
- Can ensure that everyone's job is covered by the reward criteria.
- Respect the reward recipients, because they set the standards the recipients met. Charges of favoritism disappear when employees design and judge the system.
- Have the chance to create an even playing field, where everyone has an equal opportunity to win the prizes.
- Can balance the criteria so that no part of a job suffers when a person sets his sights on a reward.
- Can keep the criteria realistic.
- Can widen the criteria to ensure that everyone who does a good job is recognized.

Did you notice one difference in terminology between the list of complaints and the list of benefits from employee involvement? The first talked primarily about "awards" and the second about "rewards." That is more than a semantic difference. Awards are conferred or bestowed; they are outside the control of the recipients. Rewards are earned; by their behavior the recipients control them.

Your employees' chief responsibility is to make sure that the reward system meets their needs. Yours is to make sure that it meets the needs of the organization.

SO WHAT'S THE MANAGER'S ROLE IN ALL THIS?

Does this mean that the manager should just abdicate authority? Or give up the right and obligation to direct behaviors and output in the work unit? Not at all. No manager can delegate the responsibility for ensuring that the reward system supports the values and goals of the organization and the objectives of the work unit.

Before you invite your employees' input into the system, you need to define your own goals and set a number of parameters. Use the checklist that follows to help you get ready.

DEVELOPING A FORMAL REWARD SYSTEM: MANAGER'S CHECKLIST

Before enlisting your employees' input in creating a reward system, you need to be prepared. Have you:

☐ Identified the organizational values and goals and departmental objectives you want the system to support?

☐ Determined what outputs from your department would support those values and objectives?

☐ Selected the best balance between behavior-based and output-based rewards?

☐ Identified nonnegotiable behaviors? For example, if your unit provides support on demand to customers or another department during specified hours, you may need to screen out or modify any reward criteria that tolerate lateness.

☐ Established a budget for the system?

☐ Considered the degree to which the system should focus on exceptional versus routine tasks? Many reward systems are dedicated to recognizing efforts above and beyond individuals' job descriptions. But employees are often demotivated because they feel underappreciated for doing their regular jobs.

☐ Ascertained the new behaviors and outputs you want the system to encourage?

☐ Researched successful reward systems in other organizations or other parts of your organization and determined what elements of those systems would work in your unit?

☐ Determined the best way to involve employees in designing the system? Will you get their written recommendations, bring them all together in meetings, or create a design team of representative employees? If your work unit is small enough, consider involving everyone. If you must select a team, make sure it is truly representative of all functions and levels in your unit.

☐ Established a schedule for designing the system?

The tasks included in the checklist are all preparatory to actually designing and implementing the reward system. Some decisions, like the balance between behavior-based and output-based rewards, will probably be up for discussion and modification by the employee team. Others, like the objectives and the budget, are likely to be nonnegotiable. You can delegate some of the tasks, like the research into other systems, but you'll have to do most of the others yourself.

Even with heavy employee involvement, you'll still have plenty more to do when the design and implementation of the system get under way. Be prepared to:

- Coach your employees on their roles in the process.
- Share your information, your parameters, and your own ideas and preferences.

John Alden Risk Management Services of Miami presents Top Rung Awards to employees who accomplish something extraordinary within their regular jobs, such as examining an unusually high number of claims.

(continues)

Employees can also earn Extra Mile Awards for extraordinary accomplishments outside their normal jobs. Such an award might go, for example, to volunteer members of a cross-department project team.

- Facilitate the planning sessions.
- Keep the group's sights on the goal—a system that supports the organization's values and objectives.
- Ensure that the system does not become so inclusive that its impact is diluted. (If everybody gets every reward, no reward will mean much.)
- Reward the system designers for their efforts and results.
- Support your employees as they work toward the rewards they define. Give feedback, assistance, and encouragement.
- Act as press agent for your reward system and your reward winners throughout the organization. Send announcements to your boss, your peers, even the president. Get articles into your company newsletter. Get your employees all the recognition they deserve!

COMPONENTS OF A REWARD SYSTEM

To be workable, the reward system you and your employees design should include:

- A list of rewards for which employees are eligible
- Reward criteria: requirements for earning each reward
- The time period for each reward
- The process for selecting recipients
- Identification of people who will select recipients
- The process for presenting rewards
- Accompanying ceremonies and celebrations

EXERCISE 3
GETTING STARTED

Start your preparatory work now by answering these three questions. They are the basis for your other decisions and recommendations to your employee-designers.

1. What organization values and goals and department objectives do you want the system to support? _____

    _____

    _____

    _____

    _____

2. What outputs from your department would support those values and objectives? _____

    _____

    _____

    _____

    _____

3. What behaviors by your employees would support organization values and contribute to department objectives? _____

    _____

    _____

    _____

    _____

Your reward system needs to reinforce these things.

GUIDELINE 2

SPECIFY REWARD CRITERIA

Knowing that her employees felt overworked and underappreciated, a manager announced a new award: dinner and theater tickets for two, to be presented to one employee each month. The first month, to no one's surprise, the award went to an employee who had brought in a half-million-dollar contract.

Over the next few months, the manager found reasons to give the award to a different employee each month. But eventually it was difficult to pick out a monthly winner. To employees, it began to look as if the award was just making the rounds. To the manager, it looked as if no one cared enough about the award to put in the extra effort that would really earn it. So after a while the idea petered out and no one missed it very much.

While it lasted, the award had some positive characteristics. Anyone could win it; it went to both professionals and support personnel. The recipients enjoyed it, while others didn't resent the winners because the award was not large, lasting, or public. And, at least at first, it felt like a genuine expression of appreciation from the manager.

What it lacked were criteria for choosing each month's recipient. Once the obvious choices were made, it was hard for the manager to pick a new recipient each month and even harder for an employee with a routine job to figure out a way to win it. So while it served as a nice thank-you for a few people, it did little to motivate improved performance because candidates did not know what was required to earn it.

In this situation, the outcome was fairly benign. The award faded away, and things went back to the way they'd always been, with no one harboring hard feelings. But in some situations, especially if the reward is significant and the candidates are competitive, the effects of fuzzy reward criteria can be seriously damaging.

CHARGES OF FAVORITISM OR LUCK

When the reward criteria are unclear, employees will work out their own reasons why a coworker earns a reward. Looking at the evidence from their point of view, it's easy to see why, when better information is unavailable, the two most common explanations are favoritism and luck.

Without published criteria, the person most likely to win is the one who's been able to read the manager's preferences and perform accordingly all along. Often such a person has a closer relationship with the manager and gets better assignments than do coworkers. Other employees, whose efforts don't seem to pay off so well, look at that relationship and see a "teacher's pet."

Alternatively, when all other explanations are unsatisfactory, people may attribute a coworker's success to being in the right place at the right time. "Who could have guessed that what they'd look for this year would be a product improvement? Randy sure lucked into that one." Randy himself will probably contribute to the impression. When he's asked how he won, he'll murmur modestly, "Just luck, I guess."

Whether the consensus of opinion is favoritism or luck, the negative impact is the same. Employees are demotivated because they can't determine the connection between effort and reward. They may even believe that the criteria are known to a select group, from which they are excluded, which only undermines their sense of competence and self-esteem.

Even when the winner's achievement is clear and worthy, other workers may feel frustrated. If they attribute the reward requirement to product improvement, to continue

It's not just special rewards that require specific criteria. How many of your employees know precisely what changes in behavior and output would boost their performance appraisal ratings from "satisfactory" to "above average" or to "excellent"?

our example, those not in the business of improving products will feel as excluded as if they had attributed Randy's success to favoritism.

EXERCISE 4
WHAT ARE YOUR CRITERIA FOR RECOGNIZING AND REWARDING EMPLOYEES?

In the left column, list the ways in which you recognize and reward the people who report to you. Include everything from pats on the back to lunch with the boss to Employee of the Month or similar awards. Then, in the right column, list the criteria you use to select recipients.

Rewards	Criteria Used

An inexpensive reward based on very specific criteria has helped ABC Home Health Care Services of Brunswick, Georgia, save $300,000 a year in workers' compensation claims and premiums. Each agency that reports no on-the-job injuries for six months receives a commendation for the office and a $10 bonus for each employee.

It's OK to include one or two spontaneous rewards based solely on what feels right at the time. But if these make up the bulk of your list, your reward pattern gives no direction to employees and may be demotivating to some.

WHAT SHOULD THE CRITERIA BE?

The answer to this question depends upon your answers to questions in Guideline 1. What are your values, and what behaviors and outcomes support those values and contribute to those objectives? Those behaviors and outcomes should be specified in your criteria. You also need to make sure that the criteria create an even playing field so that all employees, whatever their functions, have an equal opportunity to meet the requirements for the reward. A reward for saving money may inspire some creative cost-cutting among employees who have authority over choice of vendors, materials, and equipment. But it might exclude other employees who don't have such discretionary power.

In general, some popular bases for rewards are:

- Customer satisfaction
- Work quality
- Problem solving
- Work quantity
- Setting and achieving objectives
- Improving work processes
- Attendance
- Acquiring new skills

Making these specific may mean tailoring them not only to your work unit but even to the individuals within it. You could offer rewards for improving work processes, for example, and then sit down with each employee to determine what processes the employee has control over, what improvements are needed, and what this employee might do to

When you establish reward criteria, one size doesn't necessarily fit all.

qualify for the award. When you establish reward criteria, one size doesn't necessarily fit all, especially for noncompetitive awards for which everyone who meets the criteria is a winner.

SETTING GOALS

When individuals or teams are competing against a standard, not each other, there's no reason why the standard can't be defined separately for each of them. Basing rewards on individual goals produces the most precise criteria. Throughout Communicare, a health care company in Cincinnati, employees set monthly goals, which are tracked during a four-week cycle. At the end of that time their accomplishments are acknowledged in accountability sessions between employees and managers.

When employees have personal work goals with measurable standards, they can't complain about not knowing what to do. The key word here is *measurable*. That's fairly easy to achieve when the goal is quantifiable: Produce x number of widgets; reduce errors by 20 percent; increase sales by a specified number of dollars. It's trickier when the goal is more subjective, such as to improve quality. That's when you need to be absolutely certain that you and each employee have the same understanding of what constitutes successful accomplishment of the goal. Otherwise, you'll have some disappointed people on your hands when reward time comes around.

You want to avoid a conversation like this:

Employee: I don't understand why I'm not eligible for the quality award. I met my goal of training everyone to use the new spreadsheet.

Manager: But their accounting errors haven't decreased. The point of the training was to reduce errors.

Employee: But they could all do it correctly in class. I can't help it if they won't do it on the job.

With no measurement specified in the goal, the employee and manager only assumed that they were operating under the same criteria for success. When you and your employee set goals together, you need to carefully compare your mental pictures of what success will look like. Make sure they are in sync.

EXERCISE 5
SETTING MEASURABLE GOALS

Which of the five goals given below are acceptable? Answer yes if you think the goal is clear and measurable, and no if you think it is open to interpretation. If you answer no, write down the missing ingredient that would clear up the problem.

Example: Increase the number of satisfied customers by 10 percent.
Measurable? No
What's missing? A definition of *satisfied customer.*

1. Keep absenteeism in the mail room to under 5 percent for the first quarter of the year.
    Measurable? _____
    What's missing? _____

2. Significantly reduce the time required to process equipment requisitions.
    Measurable? _____
    What's missing? _____

3. Become competent in using the new database software.
    Measurable? _____
    What's missing? _____

4. Bring in four new substantial customers.
    Measurable? _____
    What's missing? _____

5. Train two people so that they are operating the X-20 machine with zero defects by July of this year.
Measurable? _____
What's missing? _____

Answers

1. *Measurable?* Yes

2. *Measurable?* No
   What's missing? Definitions of *significantly* and *to process*. What are the beginning and end points?

3. *Measurable?* No
   What's missing? Definition of *competent*. What is the level of expertise and how will it be tested?

4. *Measurable?* No
   What's missing? Definition of *substantial*. Does it refer to the size of the customer or to the amount of the business? What numbers satisfy the requirement?

5. *Measurable?* Yes

TRACKING PROGRESS

If your reason for establishing recognition and reward programs is to improve performance, it's not enough just to set goals for your employees and then wait until reward time to see if they've met them. Managers need to keep up with employees' progress toward goals, facilitate their access to resources, and guide them toward solutions to problems that block their progress. Your objective should be to have all your employees meet their goals and earn their rewards.

GUIDELINE 3

REWARD EVERYONE WHO MEETS THE CRITERIA

To draw attention to a new priority, announce a contest with valuable prizes for the winners. Give it lots of publicity, urge everyone to participate, provide a lot of reminders during the contest period, and announce the winners with fanfare and celebration.

But, if you want to make a lasting change in behavior and performance, skip the contest. In the long run, it might do more harm than good.

Why would a contest attracting widespread participation and offering high rewards do harm? Here are three reasons:

1. *Losers.* For every winner, there are tens, hundreds, or even thousands of losers. People who threw themselves into the contest, devoted their best ideas, time, and energy to their contest entries, and came up empty-handed. What the losers learn from the process is that no matter how hard they work, their chances of being rewarded are very small. So after one or two tries, they say, "Why bother?"

2. *Unheralded supporters.* For any winner, there is likely to be an anonymous support group that goes unrecognized. Think of the classic acceptance speech line, "I want to thank Tom, Dick, and Harriet, without whom this would never have happened." There are always Toms, Dicks, and Harriets whose contributions to the winning performance don't get rewarded by the organization. What happens to their motivation?

40

3. *Post-contest letdown*. After the contest, momentum grinds to a halt. When the incentive is a one-shot prize, there is often little motivation to continue the effort once the prize is won (or lost). Even if a second contest begins immediately, the winners can't triumph again with the same entry. So employees receive incentives to chuck aside what they've just spent weeks, months, or a year developing and to start something new—just for the sake of newness.

AVOIDING THE CREATION OF LOSERS

Losers are created when one worker wins a reward at the expense of all others. When you establish criteria and then reward everyone who meets them, employees compete against goals and standards rather than against each other. They are in control of their own success. Their efforts directly determine their reward. They have themselves to thank when they earn their reward.

And they have themselves to blame if they don't. There will, of course, be some people who work hard but don't achieve their goals. A few will set personal goals that are too ambitious; others may back off from their goal-driven efforts to concentrate on a different opportunity; still others may take a wrong approach to pursuing the goal. These people will miss out on their rewards, but there are significant differences between them and contest losers:

- They know why they failed to get the reward.
- The next time the reward is offered, they can use what they've learned to improve their chances of success.
- They understand that their failure to get the reward is proof of the program's objectivity rather than evidence of its arbitrary nature. This can increase their motivation the next time around.

There's another big difference between goal-based and competition-based reward systems. The thrill of the competition is in the prospect of winning, receiving the prize, and enjoying the accolades. Goal-based systems offer another reward: the personal fulfillment of accomplishing the goal and the satisfaction of a job well done. These are often more powerful motivators than any tangible reward.

EXERCISE 6
ALTERNATIVE TO CONTESTS

In the left column are some reward programs based on contests that many companies use. In the space to the right, can you recommend an alternative, criteria-based program for each? When you are finished, compare your answers to the suggestions that follow:

Contest-Based Reward Program	**Alternative Program**
1. Employee of the Quarter	_____
	_____
2. Productivity Improvement Contest	_____
	_____
3. Salesperson of the Year	_____
	_____
4. Top Team Award	_____
	_____
5. Idea of the Month	_____
	_____

Suggested Alternatives to Contests

1. Honor all employees who are commended by customers or nominated by coworkers. Post the commendations on the bulletin board where you used to hang the picture of the Employee of the Quarter.
2. Establish measurable productivity improvement

goals for every unit, and honor all units that meet their goals.

3. Honor all salespeople who meet preset quotas.

4. Establish success criteria for each cross-functional or self-directed team, and honor all teams that meet their criteria.

5. Give a small reward for all ideas. Companies that do so find that the quality as well as the quantity of ideas increases. When you implement an employee idea, establish a measure of success and present the employee with a reward of more value when success is achieved.

ARE ALL CONTESTS BAD?

No, not totally. In their favor, it can be said that they generate excitement and spur on competitive people. Certain people get a bigger charge out of measuring their progress against that of others than against a target of their own. If you've got a bunch of such people working for you, you may need a competitive reward system to motivate them.

You can have the fun and minimize the dangers of a contest if you:

1. Spell out in detail the specifications on which the competition will be based. How will entries be judged against each other?

2. Have a variety of categories and several winners.

3. Recognize all good entries, *but*. . . .

4. Emphasize that the winner was definitely the best entry and show why. Never, never announce the winner with "It was hard to make a choice." That statement suggests an arbitrary decision, lending credence to the "luck" rationalization. It detracts from the winner's glory without making the also-rans feel any better.

5. Honor everyone who was associated with the winning entry. Give all the support people their due.

6. Schedule a follow-up with the winner six months or a year later to ensure that the winning performance continues. Give the follow-up as much publicity as you gave the victory.

HYBRID REWARD PROGRAMS

Some companies have created very successful reward systems that combine some aspects of criteria-based programs and some of competitive-based programs but don't quite fit into either category.

At John Alden Risk Management Services, management chooses the recipients of the company's Top Rung awards from employees who accomplish something extraordinary within their regular jobs and the recipients of Extra Mile awards from employees who accomplish something extraordinary outside their normal jobs. But there is no competition involved. At quarterly awards meetings, the company presents as many of these awards as it feels are warranted.

Rewards based on customer feedback are effective, even though employees can't control that feedback directly. ABC Home Health Care publishes outstanding patients' comments about outstanding employees in the company newsletter and rewards each honored employee with $10. It's a small award with a lot of impact.

What's critical when management presents discretionary awards is that there be no hint of favoritism involved and that every employee has reason to believe he could be a winner one day. To accomplish this:

1. Aggressively seek out reasons to give awards. When quiet, steady employees win awards, the positive motivational impact on the work unit is much higher than when awards go to high-profile self-promoters.
2. Get nominations from peers.
3. Give as many awards as you can find good reasons

for, but keep the requirements high enough to retain the awards' prestige.

4. Publicize every award, with emphasis on the specific reasons you presented it.

TIERED REWARD SYSTEMS

Another hybrid is the tiered system, in which every entrant wins recognition or a small reward at the lowest level, but competes with fellow entrants for increasingly fewer and more valuable awards at higher levels.

Behlen Manufacturing has both criteria-based and competitive-based levels in its quality improvement suggestion program. At the base are all employees who submit an idea for quality improvement; they win Columbus bucks, good for purchases at certain local stores. At the next level are all employees whose suggestions are implemented; they get more Columbus bucks. And they get still more if their suggestions result in cost savings for the company. In addition, Behlen also honors an Idea of the Month and an Idea of the Year. During a period of eight years, Behlen implemented several thousand employee suggestions.

The advantage of tiers is that they reward more people than do single-level, exclusive programs. They give you opportunities to recognize employees who will never reach superstar status. The danger of tiers is that the existence of higher levels can diminish the luster of lower levels. You can keep the lower-level awards from becoming booby prizes by giving them the lion's share of publicity. Play up the lowest level as a notable standard of excellence, and let the higher levels be icing on the cake.

GUIDELINE 4

RECOGNIZE BEHAVIORS AS WELL AS OUTCOMES

What gets rewarded in your organization—outcomes or behaviors?

EXERCISE 7
YOUR ORGANIZATION'S
REWARD SYSTEM

To determine the answer to this question, make a list of all the forms of recognition and rewards you can recall presenting, receiving, or observing during the past several months. Your list should range from pats on the back to raises, bonuses, and promotions on to big awards like Employee of the Year.

Next to each item, describe what the recipient did to earn it.

Finally, in the third column, classify each winning performance as behavior or outcome. For example, arriving on time every day falls under behavior. A 10 percent improvement in productivity is an outcome. Responding calmly and politely to irate customers is behavior. A 20 percent decrease in the number of complaint letters from customers is an outcome.

Recognition/Reward	What Earned It	Behavior or Outcome?
_____	_____	_____
	_____	
_____	_____	_____
	_____	
_____	_____	_____
	_____	
_____	_____	_____
	_____	
_____	_____	_____
	_____	
_____	_____	_____
	_____	
_____	_____	_____
	_____	

If your organization is like most, it probably recognizes and rewards outcomes more than behaviors. Maybe that's a fallout from our long-term romance with management by objectives, or maybe it's a by-product of the empowerment movement. From either point of view, rewarding employees for specific behaviors may give the impression of trying to

Several years ago, an IBM junior executive lost more than $10 million in a risky venture for the company. When the contrite young man offered his resignation, Tom Watson, the company's founder, replied, "You can't be serious. We've just spent $10 million educating you."

control their behavior rather than allowing them the right to choose their own methods for accomplishing their goals. Or concentrating on outcomes could be the inevitable result of our focus on the bottom line.

There's nothing wrong with rewarding outcomes. If you've classified all your rewards as outcome-based, every one of them was probably worthwhile. But if your organization skimps on recognizing desirable behavior, you are missing opportunities to improve employees' perceptions of the equity equations, to motivate them to improve their skills, work habits, and processes, and to clarify for them what behaviors the organization values.

By recognizing and rewarding employees' behavior, you can:

• Support a culture change in the organization. If you want people in your organization to find it natural to cooperate rather than compete with coworkers, to take prudent risks rather than stick to the tried and true, and to take responsibility, you must recognize such changes when you see them, not wait for an outcome to occur.

• Sustain workers' interest in and excitement about a project that has a long time frame before results occur.

• Reward employees fairly if the outcome of their efforts is negative through no fault of their own—if, for example, someone else falls down on the job or a project gets canceled because company priorities change.

• Reinforce behavior changes made by unsatisfactory or borderline performers.

MOTIVATING NONSUPERSTARS

The chapter on "Motivation" in Part I recommended using recognition and rewards to encourage performance improvement by unsatisfactory workers. If you wait for a significant change in outcome, you may never get a chance to recognize or reward the employee you want to motivate. Without reinforcement, a poor performer is unlikely to sustain a behavior change long enough to accomplish an improved outcome.

A small gift for an employee who works through lunch one day (however reluctantly), praise for correcting mistakes without being told, a nonsarcastic thank-you for arriving on time for a change—all these are rewards for small behavior shifts. An employee who receives reinforcement for one change may try another, and then another, until all of them add up to the performance improvement you are looking for. Eventually you may get an outcome worthy of celebration.

A BAKER'S DOZEN OF BEHAVIORS WORTH RECOGNIZING

- Learning new skills
- Pitching in to help a coworker
- Mediating a conflict
- Volunteering for grunge work
- Giving a customer extra attention
- Mentoring a new employee
- Tackling a problem in a fresh way
- Making people laugh in a stressful situation
- Sharing information
- Taking notes in a meeting
- Perfect attendance
- Adapting willingly to change
- Cross-training another employee

. . . and all the other behaviors mentioned throughout this book.

EXERCISE 8
RECOGNIZING YOUR
EMPLOYEES' EFFORTS

What have your employees done recently that deserves recognition even if they don't yet have outstanding outcomes to show for their efforts? If you think about it, you can probably come up with at least one situation for each employee in which the person put forth more effort than usual. How did you reward that effort? If you didn't recognize it at the time, what could you do now?

Employee	Behavior	Recognition or Reward

GUIDELINE 5

SPIN THE GOLDEN RULE

Figuring out how to recognize people for good work shouldn't be hard, right? Just put yourself in their shoes and think about what you'd like as a reward. That's what a lot of the management literature advises: Treat other people the way you would like to be treated.

Unfortunately, it's not always that simple.

WHAT'S WRONG WITH THESE PICTURES?

Situation 1: An administrative assistant worked through the weekend to prepare a package of presentation materials for the boss to use in a meeting with a potential client. In typing the materials, she discovered and corrected some numerical errors that would have made the boss look very foolish. Knowing that the assistant was shy and too modest to toot her own horn, the boss held a surprise ceremony for her at a staff meeting. Everyone toasted the assistant and insisted, despite her protests, that she make a speech about what she had done. She said little and slipped out of the meeting quickly, insisting she had work to finish up. The next day the assistant called in sick.

What went wrong? _____

_____

Situation 2: A production team put forth an extraordinary effort to meet a deadline for shipping a new product.

51

To show them how much the company valued their efforts, the manager arranged to have the company president take them to lunch in the executive dining room. The morning of the lunch, the manager overheard another worker teasing one member of the production team who was dressed up for the big lunch. "I can't wait to get out of this monkey suit," the team member responded, "but while you lucky guys go out for pizza we have to sit around upstairs and listen to the stuffed shirts spout off about how we're fulfilling the strategic mission."

What went wrong? _____

_____

Situation 3: As a reward for her superb handling of a complicated project, the manager delegated an especially interesting new assignment to a team leader. The manager overheard this response when a coworker stopped by to congratulate the team leader on her good fortune: "You think this assignment is good fortune?" the person retorted. "Then you do it. It seems to me that all you get around here in return for your efforts is more work. How am I going to tell my family it's back to late nights and weekends in the office?"

What went wrong? _____

Situation 4: Another manager behaved quite differently from the one in Situation 3 when an employee did exceptional work. Instead of giving the person another task to start on, the manager gave him a week off in gratitude. Every day that week, the employee showed up and hung around looking anxious and annoying others by meddling in their work.

What went wrong? _____

Situation 5: A manager worked hard to win a promotion for an excellent employee whose opportunities had

> **Do not do unto others as you would that they should do unto you. Their tastes may not be the same.**
>
> **—GEORGE BERNARD SHAW**

seemed limited owing to restructuring and a reduction in management ranks. The new job meant greatly expanded responsibilities in a new facility on the other side of town. The manager was shocked when the employee expressed reluctance about accepting the new position. "I don't know," the employee said, "I like what I do here. All my friends are here. And that building is more than an hour away from where I live." The manager considered the employee ungrateful and began to question the person's future with the company.

What went wrong? _____

_____

In each of the five situations, the manager used a reward you'll find recommended in any text on motivating workers, including this one. The first manager praised the employee publicly. (You've heard that one a hundred times: Praise in public, criticize in private.) The second manager arranged for the employees to have exposure to upper management. The third manager offered interesting work, and the fourth an opportunity for well-earned rest and relaxation. In the fifth case, the manager arranged for the most coveted reward of all, a promotion.

So what went wrong? By now you've figured out that the answer is basically the same for all five situations. When choosing rewards, the managers failed to consider the wants and needs of the employees to be rewarded. Very likely, the managers asked themselves what *they* would like from their bosses in the same circumstances and assumed that the person to be rewarded would be delighted to get the same thing.

ONE PERSON'S FISH MAY BE ANOTHER'S POISON

The value of a reward is in the perception of the receiver. And what one person considers rewarding, another may find punishing. A number of issues, some innate and some circumstantial, affect our reactions:

• *Personality.* In Situation 1, the manager knew that the administrative assistant was very shy. That should have been a hint that she might not enjoy being thrown into such a vivid spotlight. Does this mean you should never publicly recognize a shy person? Of course not. Many people who are too shy to seek attention love it when it comes unexpectedly. What it does mean is that it's a good idea to check before forcing people into situations that may be awkward or distressing to them.

• *Trade-offs.* To get a presidential thank-you, the production team had to put up with razzing from coworkers, the loss of personal time (lunch with their friends), and uncomfortable clothes and environment. The manager would have been better advised to invite the president down to the shop floor to deliver a personal thank-you, then to take the team out for a relaxed lunch. But there are no hard-and-fast rules to guide you here. It would be a mistake to conclude from Situation 2 that no blue-collar workers like mixing with executives. The best guideline in a case like this is to give choices.

• *Work/family balance.* At what point does work begin to infringe unacceptably on personal life? That varies from individual to individual. And for any one person, it can change depending on the particular life phase one is in. When you "reward" someone with an assignment that will require extra hours or unusual travel, make it an offer that it's OK to refuse. Better yet, give the person an opportunity to design a project to fit her own lifestyle.

• *Motivational drives.* As you read Situation 4, you probably thought that the rewards in situations 3 and 4 should have been switched. Then the latter employee could have plunged happily into a new project. What the manager in Situation 4 failed to take into consideration was the individual's need for achievement. The manager's well-meaning gift of free time merely separated him from what he liked best. Situation 5 also illustrates the importance of personal needs. The manager ignored the employee's social drive. Personal relationships on the job were part of what had inspired this individual's outstanding performance.

WHAT'S A MANAGER TO DO?

Short of mind reading, how is a manager supposed to figure out what reward will please a person and what might do harm? Following are some specific suggestions and some guidelines that should help keep you out of trouble.

1. *Ask.* That's the most obvious solution. Privately tell the person that you are very pleased with his work and explain the reward you had in mind, making it clear that your idea is not yet cast in stone. Let the person know that what you really want is to give him something he values. Then ask for a reaction to your proposal.

The biggest drawback is that the person may not be willing to respond honestly to your suggestion. What you mean as an offer may be perceived as an edict, something the person must endure. Some workers find that it is better never to say no to the boss.

2. *Give options.* If you give a few suggestions, the employee can pick one without fear of offending you.

3. *Observe.* What makes the person smile? What does the individual take pleasure in during the work day? What does she talk about during her free time?

4. *Confirm your observations.* Sometimes it is appropriate to ask a good friend of the individual or even to call up a close family member.

5. *Avoid anything that might embarrass the person.* You should know an individual very well before presenting a joke award, staging a ceremonial "roast," putting the person on the spot with a call for a speech, or even asking the person to describe her accomplishments to upper management.

6. *If you don't get the desired response to your reward, do not make judgments about the employee's lack of gratitude or commitment to the organization.* How the person responds to your show of appreciation doesn't change the fact that he did a good job and is capable of doing so again. As long as the person is in the right job, someone whose pleasure at work comes from camaraderie with coworkers can be just as productive as someone with a strong desire to move up the corporate ladder.

7. *Don't be reluctant to try again if your first reward doesn't inspire cartwheels.* You won't lose face by asking, "How can I show my appreciation in a way that is more meaningful to you than last time when I put you on the spot in front of everybody?"

As the title of this chapter suggests, when it comes to recognizing and rewarding employees, you need to spin the Golden Rule a little. Here's how it should read:

> Do unto others as others would have you do unto them.

EXERCISE 9
TAILORING REWARDS TO
FIT YOUR EMPLOYEES

Go back to Exercise 8 in Guideline 4, where you identified behaviors by your employees that deserved recognition. Review your ideas for recognizing and rewarding them for their efforts. Are these the most appropriate rewards for each employee? What do you know and what should you find out about each employee that could influence your decisions? Make notes here if you think another reward is more appropriate or if you need to check out your assumptions first.

Employee	New Ideas About Rewards
_____	_____
	_____
	_____
_____	_____
	_____
	_____
_____	_____
	_____
	_____
_____	_____
	_____
	_____
_____	_____
	_____
	_____
_____	_____
	_____
	_____
_____	_____
	_____
	_____
_____	_____
	_____

GUIDELINE 6

SAY "THANK YOU" FREQUENTLY

"Why should I say 'thank you' to workers for just doing their jobs?" You've heard this before and maybe even said it yourself. It's not an uncommon attitude among managers. Yet these same people automatically say "thanks" when someone passes them the bread at the dinner table. Doing so is just good manners.

What does this attitude say to employees? People who have been brought up to say and hear "thank you" in response to the smallest act of service never hear the words on the job. If you want to draw conclusions from that, you'd have to say that doing one's job is of less value to society than passing the bread or taking out the garbage. Is that the message managers want to send?

WHY IT'S HARD TO SAY "THANK YOU"

Whatever message they want to give, some managers just find it hard to say "thank you." Their reluctance may stem from a number of different factors. Here are four common ones:

1. Saying "thank you" is not in the family tradition—the company "family," that is. We learn social manners at the knees of our parents; we learn business manners across the desk from our earliest managers. So when we reach that exalted position ourselves, we behave as our role models did.
2. Employees don't work for their managers personally, goes one line of reasoning, they work for the company,

so it's the company's job to say "thank you." The company does this with a paycheck, and that's enough. This one's a twist on the old "it's not my job" syndrome.

3. There's an argument that goes, "If I show appreciation, they'll only demand more money." But why would this happen unless the organization is trying to convince its workers that they are inadequate as an excuse for underpaying them? In fact, employees who feel very appreciated often work contentedly for less money.

4. Some managers are afraid they'll appear patronizing. And, in fact, some workers protest that they don't want to be thanked every time they do something right. They too say that they are just doing their job. (Remember, they were brought up in the family tradition too.) Yet they applaud their favorite athletes every time they score, and aren't they just doing *their* job?

When employees claim that they don't want to be thanked for doing their regular jobs, it may be because "thanks" often sounds as if the manager just noticed them for the first time. "Don't thank me for just doing my job" really means "Don't you know I do this all the time?"

SMALL WORDS, BIG IMPACT

In an organization where all four of these factors are realities, it may take a cultural revolution to introduce "thank you" as a meaningful form of recognition. But it is worth the effort to derive the benefits.

Benefit one. A thank-you validates the importance of the work people do. Since we were brought up to show our appreciation by saying "thank you," the logical line of thinking is: "no thanks . . . not appreciated . . . not worth doing."

Benefit two. Thank-you is always ready for use. With it

you can give timely recognition, immediately reinforcing behaviors you want the employee to repeat. We punish undesired behavior the minute we see it, knowing that delayed punishment has no effect, but we wait until the end of the year to reward people with a raise or a bonus. Memory, however, can be pretty murky. Months later, it's hard to pinpoint just what behaviors are being rewarded.

Benefit three. Thank-you is one reward you can afford to give for partial success. You can motivate people to do a task by rewarding incremental improvements as the person performs in a way that approximates the desired behavior. Few managers can give a bonus each time an employee arrives 10 minutes closer to the mandated 9 A.M. But the manager can say "Thanks for arriving earlier than you did yesterday. I'm sure you'll be here at nine tomorrow."

Does this mean that you should say "Thanks for finishing twelve letters out of the pile of fifteen I gave you to do. The rest don't really matter." Not at all. Use your thank-you's more pointedly, to reinforce what was done right: "Thanks for doing a good job on the Johnson and Brown letters. I'm hoping to get some important new accounts with them." Follow this up the next morning with, "It's really important that all the letters go out today, so they are as timely as the Johnson and Brown letters you did yesterday."

Benefit four. Just as you can use a thank-you to recognize incremental improvements in performance that would never rate a major reward, you can also use it to show your appreciation of routine work. Most rewards are for performance above and beyond the call of duty; but where would you be if your employees weren't doing their duties? Don't they deserve recognition for their routine contributions to your success?

Benefit five. Generous use of thanks is contagious. As people begin to realize that it feels good to be on both the giving and the receiving end of it, more people will use it more often, boosting morale and good relationships throughout your work unit.

The person who works well four days out of five ought to be praised four times as often as he's dumped on. But guess what. That's exactly the opposite of what happens. The 80 percent

(continues)

of the time that he works well will simply go without comment because that's what he's supposed to be doing.

—**FRAN TARKENTON** Former National Football League star quarterback, from his book *How to Motivate People*

EXERCISE 10
SAYING "THANK YOU" FOR ROUTINE WORK

Think of a mundane, routine, and utterly critical task done by each of your employees. List these tasks here to remind yourself to acknowledge the importance of this work by saying "thank you."

Employee	Task
_____	_____
_____	_____
_____	_____
_____	_____
_____	_____
_____	_____
_____	_____
_____	_____
_____	_____
_____	_____
_____	_____

SAYING "THANK YOU" SO IT MOTIVATES

When you thank your employees, you will underline the importance of their work and your appreciation of their efforts if you follow these three guidelines:

1. Be specific about the behavior you are recognizing with your thanks. For example:

   Thank you for smiling at each customer and remaining calm even on hectic days. I know it gets hard sometimes, and I appreciate your willingness to stick it out each day.

"Thanks for a great job" isn't good enough. Anyone can say that, even someone who hasn't the slightest idea what work the employee has done.

2. Tell the employee why the behavior is important to you and the organization.

Your helpfulness and good cheer keep our customers coming back. Our business depends on return customers.

3. Be immediate. Thank your employees on the spot; don't wait for a staff meeting or a more opportune moment, such as a time when everyone is less busy. (You can say "thank you" at those times, too, but give those thanks in addition to the spontaneous ones.)

Thank you for staying calm with that customer. I appreciate that you kept smiling despite the customer's rudeness.

EXERCISE 11
WHAT ARE YOU GOING TO SAY?

In Exercise 10, you identified tasks you want to thank your employees for doing. Here, plan *how* you will say thanks, being specific and spelling out why the task is important. Note also *when* you will say it so as to make it as timely as possible.

Employee   **What You Will Say and When**

_____   _____

                              _____

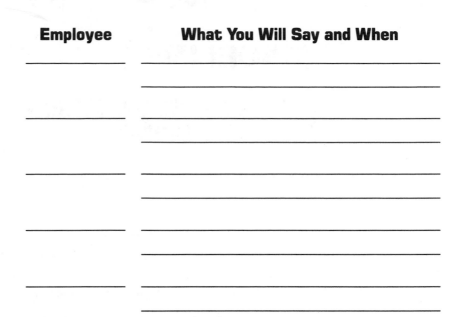

Employee	What You Will Say and When

Bosses and Peers Need It, Too

Thank-you isn't just for people who report to you. It's the reward you have the power and the resources to give to your boss and your peers in the organization when they do something of value to you. It's also a tool for influencing changes in their behavior. By thanking them specifically when you catch them doing something that is helpful to you, you give them the information and motivation they need to continue behaving in a way that's best for you.

Your boss needs to be appreciated just as much as your employees—and you—do.

GUIDELINE 7

NURTURE SELF-ESTEEM AND BELONGING

Consider the cases of two employees who started work together in a big company. They had similar backgrounds and skills, and both joined the firm full of enthusiasm, with expectations of exciting, successful careers.

A few years later, Employee A was well on the way to turning those expectations into reality. This employee had a track record of applying innovative solutions to problems and looked forward confidently to every new challenge.

Employee B, on the other hand, had settled into a routine job and lived in fear of losing that if the company downsized. Turned down for a promotion, Employee B wasn't surprised. "I didn't really expect to get it," this employee told a friend.

Working in the same company, how did Employee A develop into a self-confident go-getter while B shriveled into a person with low self-esteem and few prospects? If you could study a videotape of their years on the job, you'd see a noticeable difference in the way they were managed.

You'd see Employee A's first manager introducing him to the work unit as a person of great potential who was a valuable addition to the department. And you would see Employee B, on the first day, being silently led to a desk and given the employee handbook to read.

You'd see Employee A being invited to contribute ideas from the start and having those ideas treated with interest and respect. You'd see B's manager suggesting that B would better understand how the organization functioned by watching and listening.

You'd see both getting the lowliest tasks to do at the outset, but you'd also see Employee A's manager thanking A for doing them well and explaining how important they were to the success of the project. But you would see Employee B's manager accepting B's work with no comments.

As time went on, you'd see A earning praise and recognition for innovative work. But the only recognition you'd see B getting would be negative feedback when occasionally something went wrong.

Cycle of Defeat

Over time, people whose best efforts go unrecognized and apparently unappreciated begin to buy into the negative perception of what others think of them. When this happens, their work reflects their reduced expectations for themselves.

It's hard to say exactly what's cause and what's effect in the negative cycle that results. It's entirely possible that if pressed for an assessment, Employee B's first manager would have told an outsider that B was a fine worker. But never hearing this and getting no opportunities to shine, Employee B was destined to lose confidence and develop a negative self-image. As B's work shrank to match that self-image, the manager's actual assessment of the employee took a nose-dive, too, until it paralleled what B perceived it to be. By that time, both employee and employer took it for granted that B's prospects were limited—and so they were.

GIVING POSITIVE FEEDBACK

Employee B, unfortunately, worked for a manager who had never mastered the art of giving positive feedback, the form of recognition that has the biggest impact on employees' self-esteem. Assess your own managerial skills below. As you read the following guidelines, check those you are confident you accomplish when you give positive feedback to your employees. Are you:

☐ *Specific?* Specific feedback tells the employee exactly what facets of his work are really important to the company, gives information he can use to focus his efforts even more productively, and indicates that you are paying attention and that you care.

☐ *Realistic?* There is such a thing as laying it on too thick, and employees will recognize this—and discount it. "With your drive and enthusiasm there's no reason you can't be making $100,000 in commissions next year" is less effective than "Your timing in closing the sale today was excellent. You picked right up on the slight change in the prospect's voice that showed she was ready to buy."

☐ *Consistent in your treatment of all your employees?* Singling out just one employee for compliments makes both that person and her colleagues uncomfortable.

☐ *Consistent with your known style?* Employees will distrust a manager who has been niggardly with compliments in the past and then suddenly starts showering people with verbal bouquets. If you are new to this, start off low-key, and be very specific.

☐ *Faithful about follow-up?* There are both small ways and large ways to reinforce your feedback with follow-up. If you see a magazine article that's pertinent to the employee's accomplishment, make sure the employee gets a copy. If management holds a meeting on the same or a similar subject, take the employee along. If you can get the employee on the agenda as a speaker, that's better yet.

Recognition → Self-esteem → Performance

When people are recognized for their potential, their efforts, and their accomplishments, there's a high likelihood they will develop into employees who:

- Set challenging goals for themselves.
- Find innovative ways to meet those goals.
- Overcome setbacks, because they assume they can.
- Continually seek new opportunities.
- Enjoy responsibility and managing their own work.

Without recognition, it takes unusually thick skin and exceptional inner drive for an employee not to:

- Feel inadequate and thus resist challenges.
- Stick with what's familiar and low-risk.
- Blame herself when things go wrong (often covered up by blaming others).
- Hide mistakes.
- Look for direction from others.

GAINING THE ESTEEM OF OTHERS

The way we see ourselves is largely a reflection of the way others see us. Because of this, it's very hard for an employee to maintain a sense of self-worth if he is not held in esteem by his managers and peers. It is also very difficult for such a person to:

- Get the necessary resources and cooperation to perform well.
- Grow in the organization.
- Participate productively in team efforts.

If others have low regard for an individual because that person is a poor performer, then performance is the manager's first problem. But there are many other reasons, some subtle and some insidious, why some individuals fail to enjoy the esteem of their coworkers and management. This uncomfortable situation may exist because:

- *The person is simply too quiet to be noticed.* The problem isn't necessarily negative regard, but rather no regard at all. This person often gets overlooked.

- *There is a personality clash.* A team of extroverts may jump to the conclusion that a serious, reserved person is standoffish and not a team player.
- *The person's job is considered insignificant.* Thus a support person may be held in less esteem than a professional.
- *The employee's coworkers focus on one or two negatives.* Perhaps the person once made a mistake that caused them all a problem, after which they failed to appreciate the individual's positive qualities.
- *Colleagues are jealous.* There's such a thing as too much fanfare. If a person joining a group is too highly touted, the others may band together against this individual (particularly if they think his reputation is undeserved).
- *In a really bad environment, where everyone feels insecure, there is often a pecking order.* The person may be on the bottom simply by virtue of having the least seniority or the lowliest position.

By giving the right kind of recognition to both the individual held in low regard and to the rest of the group, the manager can improve the way others view the slighted individual. The accompanying checklist suggests things a manager can do to provide appropriate recognition.

But remember, singling out one person for recognition can backfire if others have strong grievances (real or imagined) against that person. You can guard against this by spreading your recognition around, making sure that everyone gets a fair share. Doing the things on the checklist on an ongoing basis for all your employees will help maintain morale and mutual respect among everyone in your work unit.

BUILDING EMPLOYEES' SELF-ESTEEM AND ESTEEM IN THE EYES OF OTHERS

Check those things that you've done for at least one employee during the past month.

☐ 1. Acknowledge the entire team for a team success, specifying the contributions of each, including the contributions made by the employee whose esteem needs boosting.

☐ 2. Send a note to your boss detailing an accomplishment by the employee and also a copy to the employee.

☐ 3. Circulate a memo detailing the employee's accomplishment to everyone on your team, emphasizing this person's contribution to the team's success.

☐ 4. For a new person, publicly recognize her qualifications that can contribute most to your team's success.

☐ 5. Put the individual on a small team project, on which the person's contributions are important to the project's success.

☐ 6. Enlist the help of a "plant." Get someone who is respected by all to acknowledge specifically the individual's efforts and outputs, focusing on how they have contributed to the success of the whole group.

☐ 7. At a staff meeting, ask each person to report one thing every other person there has done recently that helped the person who is reporting.

☐ 8. At a staff meeting, acknowledge one thing every person there has done recently that helped you personally.

☐ 9. Let the individual choose an assignment from a list of options, all of which involve working with others.

☐ 10. Take your employees, one at a time, to meetings with your boss. Schedule the person with low esteem high, but not first, on your list.

And don't forget to say "thank you" regularly.

EXERCISE 12
WHAT WOULD YOU DO?

What methods of recognition could you use to help solve the problems that follow? Choose techniques from the preceding checklist or be creative and think up some of your own.

A. Chris has been a manager for several months in a research and development facility. Chris thinks Robert, a researcher, is being underutilized. He does routine work well, but seems to work in the shadow of his more experienced fellow researchers, who tend to shut him out of high-profile assignments. When Chris assigned an important role in a project to Robert, the senior researchers each came to Chris and objected, saying they were afraid Robert couldn't handle it and would let them down. Chris insisted that Robert have the opportunity, but the others have infringed on Robert's assignment, taking over his tasks one by one. Rather than stand up for himself, Robert has fallen back into his old role of doing the grunt work for the project team. Chris brought the issue up with the head of the facility, whose response was, "I don't know who this Robert is."

B. Lee is the manager of a very close-knit work group in a company that has had some business failures in the past few years. One of these failures involved a product that was introduced with much fanfare, but flopped. Lee was asked to take on Jill, an employee who had been part of that high-profile product team. "Jill did good work, but she's feeling pretty low right now," Lee's boss said. "I'm confident that in your group she can bounce back." Unfortunately, when they heard that Jill was joining them, Lee's employees expressed resentment. "We may all be losing our jobs soon, and now we've got to shelter someone who helped cause that disaster," one of them complained. They've pretty much closed ranks against Jill, although she willingly takes on even menial tasks to help the group.

C. Jenny, an administrative assistant, was hired by Pat, the manager, as part of the company's program to help the disadvantaged. Pat didn't really have high hopes but was willing to try her out. Actually, Jenny surprised Pat by how quickly she learned the company's computer systems, but this evidence that she has ability makes her attitude almost more exasperating. She is often late with assignments and sloppy about mistakes. Jenny supports several analysts, and most of them complain about her constantly. Oddly, one analyst, Kim, seems to have no trouble with her and always has good reports about Jenny's work. In fact, twice last month, Kim sent Pat notes, with copies sent to Jenny, commending Jenny's speed and accuracy in preparing reports. Pat had hoped that Jenny would be motivated by the example when another administrative assistant received a commendation and bonus, but if anything Jenny got worse after that.

Suggested Techniques From the Checklist

A: 1, 2, 4, 5, 9, 10
B: 3, 4, 5, 7, 10
C: 1, 2, 3, 6, 8, 9

GUIDELINE 8

FOSTER INTRINSIC REWARDS

When we talk about rewards employees can earn for their work, we are usually referring to things provided by the organization, by the manager, or by others in recognition of the job done. These are *extrinsic* rewards.

But there are other kinds of rewards, which many consider much more powerful. These are *intrinsic* rewards, and they come from within the individual. Intrinsic rewards are the good feelings people get from the work itself, feelings like enjoyment from the very act of performing the tasks involved, excitement about confronting and overcoming challenges, satisfaction in helping others or accomplishing something worthwhile, and pride in doing a job well. These are the rewards that inspire missionaries and artists and theoretical scientists. And they are the rewards that keep an employee working late on a project even when there is no expectation of overtime pay.

You can pinpoint the difference between extrinsic and intrinsic rewards if you think about what you get from your own job. What tasks do you do primarily because of the money, other tangible paybacks, or praise from others for doing them? List three such tasks here:

1. _____
2. _____
3. _____

What tasks do you do primarily because of the good feelings you get from doing them? List three such tasks here:

1. _____
2. _____
3. _____

Your job, like most, probably provides you with some of both kinds of reward. Without the first, you couldn't afford to stay on the job. Without the second, you'd hate it.

WHAT CAN A MANAGER DO?

If intrinsic rewards come from within the individual, does this let the organization and the manager off the hook? Hardly. You can't hand out intrinsic rewards on Awards Night or put them in a paycheck. But, as a manager, you can do a number of things to create an environment in your work unit where:

- Work is more fun. Yes, fun. It's not a dirty word.
- Employees know that the work they do is meaningful and worthwhile.
- Problems are viewed as challenges, not restraints.
- It's OK for employees to try new ways of doing tasks and to do new tasks that interest them.
- Employees know when they've done a good job.

In this kind of environment, workers will experience intrinsic motivation!

EXERCISE 13
PAVING THE WAY TO
INTRINSIC REWARDS

For each question below, pick the answer or answers that offer opportunities for employees to experience intrinsic rewards.

1. To make a task more fun, would you:
   a. Start a regular Friday pizza lunch for the entire work unit?
   b. Encourage people doing the task to work in small teams and to identify and implement creative new ways of accomplishing the task more effectively?
   c. Have a monthly drawing for two tickets to an evening's entertainment?

2. To ensure that employees know that the work they do is important, would you:
   a. Give a monthly bonus to the individual or team that saves the organization the most money?
   b. Trace the outcome of their efforts beyond their own tasks, emphasizing the impact of their contributions? Fill them in on the outcomes of the letters they typed, the reports they helped write, the products they made parts for?
   c. Treat employees who do routine tasks with the same dignity and respect you show those who do high-profile, creative work?

3. To encourage employees to view problems as challenges, not as restraints, would you:
   a. Respond with interest and enthusiasm rather than with dismay and discouragement when employees come to you with problems *and* potential solutions?
   b. Give a reward to the person who comes up with the best solution to a problem?
   c. Discourage people from telling you about problems until after they are solved?

4. To demonstrate to employees that you welcome their innovations, would you:
   a. Support their ideas with resources and time

and by running interference with upper management and other work units if necessary?
   b. When new ideas don't work, look for lessons
      the employee can apply to his next innovation
      rather than punishing the person for failure?
   c. Give bonuses to employees who develop innovative approaches for doing their work
      better?

5. So that employees know when they've done a
   good job, would you:
   a. Hold periodic progress review sessions in
      which they do most of the talking?
   b. Give them high grades at performance appraisal time?
   c. Give them the tools with which to do their
      own quality control?

Answers and Analysis

The best suggestions for creating an environment in which
work is intrinsically rewarding are: 1. *b;* 2. *b, c;* 3. *a;* 4. *a, b;*
5. *a, c.* Most of the other answers are not all "bad." Some of
them are effective ways to recognize and reward employees,
but they involve extrinsic, not intrinsic, rewards. You'll see
this as we analyze each question individually.

Question 1: Answer *a,* recommending Friday pizza
lunches, is a good example of an idea that might well boost
morale in the work unit. But, although it may make Fridays
on the job more fun, it won't change the nature of the work
one bit. Nor would *c,* the monthly drawing, although that
might be a nice way to show your appreciation of the whole
group's efforts.

Only *b,* giving employees an opportunity to work together, which is often more fun than working alone, and to
be creative, which is why many people enjoy hobbies, has
the potential to make work more fun.

Question 2: Answer *a* has two strikes against it in this exercise. First, it's an extrinsic, not an intrinsic, reward. Second, since it's a prize for a competition, it does nothing to show the nonwinners that their work too is important. In fact, it may do just the opposite; after losing a few times, very able workers doing significant work may begin to get the idea that their efforts don't count.

Answers *b* and *c* are particularly important for people in support roles, who rarely get credit for the work unit's output and who too often are treated as pairs of hands rather than as thinking people with a stake in the organization's success.

Question 3: Managers who take approach *a* set an example for their employees. By their actions they give the impression that, sure this problem changes things, but it makes the project all the more interesting.

Answer *b,* like *2a,* above, is both extrinsic and exclusive. Answer *c* is just plain bad management. It's an approach that encourages employees to hide their problems, often until it's too late to solve them.

Question 4: Answer *a* involves some management tasks that pave the way for employee success as well as intrinsic rewards. These are tasks that involve "serving" the employee. If that sounds like a twist, heed the words of Max DePree, chairman of the highly admired Fortune 500 company Herman Miller, Inc., and author of an equally admired book on management, *Leadership Is an Art.* "The first responsibility of a leader is to define reality," writes DePree. "The last is to say thank you. In between, the leader is a servant."

Answer *b* reminds managers that asking for innovation but punishing people when it doesn't work sends an immobilizing mixed message. To enjoy trying new things, employees must be free of fear about outcomes.

If you have the resources to give bonuses (answer *c*), they may be an effective extrinsic reward, but they won't improve the intrinsic rewards inherent in the work itself.

Question 5: Why does answer *a* specify that employees should do most of the talking at progress review meetings? Because, by inviting employees to tell you about specific things they are doing right, you are encouraging them to draw upon their own good feelings about their work and thus reinforcing their convictions that they are doing well. To help them retain these convictions you do need to confirm them and to add your own positive feedback, as well as to help employees work out any problems that come up in the review sessions.

Answer *b,* like 4*c* above, is an extrinsic, not an intrinsic, reward, although it is an important one that got attention in an earlier chapter.

Companies that do the best job of quality control make it the responsibility of the person performing the task. When you give people the tools to control the quality of their own work (answer *c*), you are also giving them the tools to confirm for themselves that they are doing their job well.

UNLEASHING INTRINSIC REWARDS THROUGH EMPOWERMENT

With power to pursue their innovative ideas, use their best skills, and make important contributions to the organization, employees also have an increased potential for experiencing intrinsic rewards—feelings of satisfaction about their work. For many employees, power itself is an intrinsic reward.

But what's in all this for managers? Doesn't empowering employees diminish their own power? Not at all. Power is not a zero sum game. Empowered employees working creatively produce a more powerful work unit, thus increasing the power of the manager.

You can expand the power of your employees, your work unit, and yourself by:

- Giving them authority to set goals, make decisions, and solve problems.

- Helping them to obtain necessary resources.
- Facilitating their access to people (including yourself, upper management, people in other parts of the company) whose help and cooperation they need to accomplish their work.
- Providing information. If your organization is in a state of continuous change, both you and your employees may feel powerless because you don't know what is going on. You can empower yourself and your employees if you relentlessly pursue information about your company's mission, plans, financial status, and progress toward meeting its goals.

ENRICHING A JOB TO INCREASE INTRINSIC MOTIVATION

You've read advice about making mundane jobs more interesting through job enrichment—that is, increasing the scope of the job and providing more opportunities for challenging work. All that advice is in line with this chapter's call to create an environment in which work is intrinsically rewarding. But you must be careful to distinguish between job enrichment and job loading, which merely enlarges the perceived meaninglessness of a job.

Be sure that, in the name of job enrichment, you don't just:

- Add another routine task to the existing ones. An employee who is bored with filing probably won't get satisfaction out of an additional assignment to distribute the department mail twice a day.
- Increase the amount of production expected. Don't reward an employee who can write 100 orders a day by expecting that person to write 150.
- Rotate the person to another equally boring job.

Instead, you can enrich an employee's job—and increase the likelihood that the person will find it intrinsically rewarding—by providing:

- An opportunity to handle a project from beginning to end, producing an output the employee can point to with pride and say, "I did that."
- A chance to develop new skills and demonstrate new competencies.
- Rotation to a project with high visibility in the organization.

GUIDELINE 9

REWARD THE WHOLE TEAM

One of the biggest changes in organizations in the 1990s has been the increasing emphasis on teams. Cross-functional teams, self-managed teams, high-performance teams—these have revolutionized the shape of the organization chart and the way work gets done in many of the top-ranked companies in business tody.

Inevitably, the focus on teams is also changing the way organizations reward their people. Traditional reward systems, which encourage individual achievement, are often at odds with the goals and the structure of teams.

THE PERILS IN THE OLD SYSTEM

Teams rely on cooperation. At best, individual reward systems foster the pursuit of individual achievement. At worst, if the reward system is based on the ranking of employees or the selection of a few award winners, it can act as an incentive to people to hoard information, undercut their fellow workers, and resist helping one another.

Watch for evidence of these problems as you read the following case study.

Keep Healthy Insurance Company reorganized its claims office into work teams that included claims processors, technical experts, and customer service representatives. The company expected that by putting these people together in teams, they would cooperate in find-ing better, faster ways to satisfy customers. The teams were to write their own goals, develop their own work processes, cross-train each other, and manage themselves, thus eliminating one layer of management in the office.

After some initial confusion, the teams began to make some real advances through innovative processes and by the way team members pitched in to help each other. One team went so far as to call spontaneous "tough claim" meetings to discuss any difficult or unique claim that came in. Everyone learned from the meetings, and the resulting actions on the claims were accurate and timely.

But their first biannual review under the team organiza-tion came as a shock to several of the claims proces-sors, who were paid under an incentive system that rated individuals according to the number of claims each had processed. Now, although the teams were paying more claims with greater accuracy, some of the top-rated claims processors were paying fewer claims indi-vidually. To their dismay, they found their ratings, and thus their wages, reduced. The claims processors be-gan to grumble that team activities were taking them away from their real work.

The next time a team member called a "tough claim" meeting, several of the downrated processors begged off, pointing to their backlogs. Within a week, two of them received similar claims to deal with. One asked a teammate what had been decided at the meeting. "You wouldn't come; you figure it out," the teammate replied icily. So the processor dumped the claim on the techni-cal expert, stating, "I don't have time for this." The second claims processor worked on the difficult claim and resolved it in a manner that had the customer screaming at a customer service rep in no time flat. With an ear still ringing from the phone call, the rep walked the documentation over to the processor. "This is your mess," the rep said. "You fix it. Why should I solve your problems so you can push claims through and get paid more?"

1. What undermined the good results that the teams had begun to accomplish?

        _____

        _____

2. Who suffered (and how) from the impact of the conflict between goals and rewards?

        _____

        _____

3. What does Keep Healthy Insurance Company need to do to get its teams back on track?

        _____

        _____

Answers to Case Study Questions

1. The conflict between the individual incentive system and the need to cooperate on the team.

2. Everyone: the claims processors, by having their income reduced because they were spending time on things other than directly processing claims; the technical expert, who began to receive extra work just because a particular claim was going to take more time than the processor wanted to spend on it; the customer, by receiving a poor judgment on a claim; the CSR, by having to listen to an angry complaint that could have been prevented; and, of course, the company as a whole.

3. Begin by reassessing its reward system and changing those elements that are out of sync with its new structure.

Behlen Manufacturing tracks the productivity of more than thirty work teams, linking the measurements directly to financial results. As improvement occurs, the financial rewards are shared between company and team members and paid out monthly.

SOLVING THE PROBLEM

Many experts call for eliminating individual incentives in team-based organizations and for replacing them with team rewards. There are, however, still some voices resisting a total changeover. The holdouts note that team rewards give the same treatment to all team members whether they are high or low contributors. That's almost bound to cause resentment among the high contributors while giving slackers no incentive to improve.

Organizations with well-entrenched team structures resolve this dilemma by way of a two-pronged system involving:

1. *Team rewards for meeting team goals,* as these relate to accomplishments (bottom-line results), processes (working together, sharing information, communicating across teams), and skills development (expanding the skills of the entire team). In many companies, team rewards are linked directly to the increased profitability of the team or of the organization as a whole.

2. *Individual rewards based on peer evaluations.* Team members assess each other's contributions and individual skills development. Obviously, this isn't fail-safe. There's an inherent danger of team members antagonizing each other and thereby splintering the team irreparably. But well-trained and skilled assessors use the assessment sessions as opportunities to help everyone reach full potential.

WHAT AN INDIVIDUAL MANAGER CAN DO

If you are a manager with no input into your organization's compensation system, how can you translate these recognition and reward concepts into things you can do to encourage teamwork in your work unit?

Here are five guidelines to help you put team-based rewards to work. Check those you want to concentrate on:

☐ 1. For a team effort, reward the behind-the-scenes workers in the same way you reward the more visible team spokespersons.

☐ 2. Encourage the formation of ad hoc teams by paying nominal bonuses or presenting awards to everyone who joins a team to tackle a work problem.

☐ 3. Encourage teams to write process, skill-development, and output goals. Recognize the entire team as these goals are met.

☐ 4. Make team behavior a part of the basis for every individual appraisal. Be sure that employees know this at the start of the appraisal cycle and know specifically what they have to do to get superior ratings.

☐ 5. Train employees in peer assessment and provide teams with team-member assessment tools. Encourage employees to seek their teammates' assessments both as a guide to performance improvement and as a contribution to their individual appraisals. You can start by making this voluntary on their part.

GUIDELINE 10

BE CAREFUL: YOU GET WHAT YOU REWARD

There are examples everywhere of organizations that undermine their own intentions by proclaiming one value but rewarding another, at both the organization and department level. Here are some situations you've all seen:

What the Organization Says	What Management Rewards
"We value quality."	Cutting corners to lower costs
"We believe in cooperation and teamwork."	Competing with each other internally
"We are a learning organization."	Doing things the old way
"We value diversity."	Conforming
"We want out employees to have well-rounded lives that balance work, family, and community."	Staying late at night and coming in over weekends
"We expect our customer service representatives to be courteous and caring."	Keeping customer contact brief.

RESULTS OF REWARD DISSONANCE

Outmoded or ill-advised reward systems can result in unhealthy internal competition, the undermining of coworkers, "doctoring" of the records, or mistreatment of customers. For example:

• An insurance company talks quality, quality, quality in its claims offices, but it pays its claims processors on an incentive basis that rewards them for the quantity of claims they process.

Quality or quantity, which do you think it gets? _____

• A chain of auto maintenance centers advertises excellent, economical service. But its incentive plan for managers is based on the number of parts the center sells.

What are customers likely to get: economical repairs or unnecessary new parts? _____

(What the company got was an indictment for fraud.)

• A giant corporation spends millions sending all its managers to a week-long training program to learn new leadership skills and facilitate a culture change. When the managers return to their jobs, their bosses say, "That new stuff is fine for the classroom, but back here I pay you to do things my way."

How much change is likely to happen in this organization?

• A manufacturing operation is trying to convert to a team-based structure. But it pays bonuses to the workers who produce the most units independently.

What will get highest priority, team work or individual work? _____

• A company encourages its salespeople to focus on repeat business, which is gravy for the company, but it pays higher commissions for bringing in new customers.

Which will the salespeople concentrate on, new or repeat business? _____

ASSESS YOUR OWN PRACTICES

In your work unit, are you rewarding:

A fisherman felt a bump against the side of his boat. Looking down, he saw a snake with a frog in its mouth. The fisherman grabbed his oar and whacked the snake. It dropped the frog, which swam away quickly. Then, feeling sorry for the snake, the fisherman looked around for something to give it.

(continues)

All he had was a bottle of rum, so he gave the snake a long swig. The snake swam off happily. In a few minutes, the fisherman felt another bump. There was the snake again, this time holding two frogs in its mouth.

—Adapted from a parable told by Michael LeBoeuf in *The Greatest Management Principle in the World*

- Teamwork or internal competition? _____
- Resolving problems to the customer's satis- _____
faction or getting rid of the complaint as
quickly as possible?
- Quality or quantity of output? _____
- Individual initiative or doing things your _____
way?

What rewards should you change to encourage the kinds of behavior and outcomes your organization says it wants?

PART

100 WAYS TO RECOGNIZE & REWARD PEOPLE

Although the following sections do not constitute an exhaustive list, the 100 specific suggestions given here for ways to recognize and reward people should include some that you will find useful and others that will spark new ideas of your own. Some of these have been mentioned elsewhere in the book; some you'll encounter here for the first time. Some are free (in terms of monetary cost), many have a nominal cost, and a few are fairly expensive or open-ended (the dollar amount being up to you). All of them are intended to supplement your organization's official compensation plans. Scaled up or down, they are applicable to any size work unit.

Most of the suggestions are geared for managers to give to employees, either individuals or teams. But the people who work for you aren't the only ones who deserve recognition. So some items are for coworkers, customers, and even your boss.

To make the list easier to navigate, it is divided into three sections:

1. *Structured reward programs,* including systems with prearranged criteria, schedules, and awards
2. *Spontaneous rewards,* for acknowledging exceptional performance when it happens
3. *Day-to-day feedback,* to encourage consistent performers to keep up the good work.

SECTION 1

STRUCTURED REWARD PROGRAMS

What the items on this list have in common is that they are each planned in advance, based on specified criteria, and operated according to a schedule (except for four that are ongoing). They differ in their intent: Some recognize individuals, and others teams; some are to reward performance and others to boost morale. They vary also in their "weightiness"; some are serious stuff, others lighthearted.

As you review this list and the ones in the following sections, note those you have already used and those you will use in the future (not necessarily mutually exclusive). If your "have used" count is high, you'll want to keep it up; if it's low, that might be your cue to put more checks into the "will use" column and follow up on your intent.

REWARDS FOR ACCOMPLISHING MAJOR WRITTEN GOALS

Reward	Have Used	Will Use
1. *Cash bonus upon goal accomplishment by an individual or team.* Don't wait until the end of the year when the reward's connection to the work effort has worn thin.	_____	_____
2. *Pizza or champagne party to honor an individual or team upon goal accomplishment.*	_____	_____
3. *Wall of Fame.* Keep it active for a year, adding a framed picture of each employee as he or she completes written goals.	_____	_____

Reward	Have Used	Will Use
4. *Training course or seminar to prepare person for an even more sophisticated set of goals next time.*	_____	_____
5. *Professional conference related to the individual's area of accomplishment.*	_____	_____
6. *Weekend at a country inn for individual and companion,* to be awarded upon completion of task.	_____	_____

MONTHLY, QUARTERLY, BIANNUAL, OR ANNUAL RECOGNITION EVENTS

	Have Used	Will Use
7. *Values lunch* (or breakfast or dinner) *to recognize specific behaviors by employees that support your organization's stated values.* Enlist nominations, requiring specific descriptions of behavior, in advance and recognize everyone duly nominated.	_____	_____
8. *Commendation from peers party.* Invite submissions in advance and use them all. Celebrate with cake or champagne.	_____	_____
9. *Recognition lunch honoring people for meeting short-term* (monthly, quarterly) *goals.*	_____	_____
10. *Thank-you meeting at which everyone in work unit thanks everyone else for something specific.* Hold these at regular intervals and remind people to keep track of small favors that they can mention when called upon to speak.	_____	_____
11. *Biggest Boner Award, given monthly to the person who admits to the biggest mistake.* It can be a funny trophy, but the intent is serious. In too many organizations, people are afraid to admit their mistakes, so they get covered up, not solved. The presentation event should be a problem-solving meeting, and the outcome should be a viable approach to resolving the problem. Start off by giving yourself the award and asking others' suggestions for tackling your problem. Then invite others to nominate themselves for the award next time.	_____	_____

		Have Used	Will Use
	Reward		

12. *Solution Award,* presented as a follow-up to the Biggest Boner Award when the mistake is corrected. _____ _____

13. *Suggestion plan prizes.* Reward each contributor with a chance for a monthly drawing. Have several prizes of different values each month. If you are afraid people will stuff the suggestion box with worthless ideas, you needn't worry. Organizations that pay for every suggestion regardless of whether it is implemented report that the quality of suggestions goes up, not down. You can also maintain a level of psychological control by reading aloud every suggestion that wins a prize. _____ _____

14. *Community service recognition event.* Give a certificate or plaque to everyone who fulfills a commitment to community service, pledged at the beginning of the cycle. _____ _____

15. *"Thank a Customer" party.* Everyone invites a favorite customer (external or internal) and presents a citation to the guest. Inviting guests to respond is a great way to solicit some positive feedback. _____ _____

16. *"Catch Them Doing Something Right" video.* A year's worth of on-the-job highlights captured on videotape, played at a recognition event or holiday party. Or keep it ready to play in the work unit all during the following year. _____ _____

17. *Work unit yearbook or "annual report" featuring accomplishments of all employees.* Desktop publishing makes it possible to do a professional-looking job inexpensively. Each employee gets one. Keep yours prominently displayed in your office. _____ _____

CONTESTS

18. *"Who can do the most (fill in the blank) in a week?" contest.* One appropriate prize: The manager washes the winner's car in the company parking lot. Yes, despite the dangers of competitive rewards, occasional contests can boost performance and morale. Keys to success: a level playing field on which

Reward	Have Used	Will Use
everyone starts with a perceived equal chance of winning; a short duration; and a prize that's worth competing for, but is not an incentive to coworkers to undercut each other, or likely to cause jealousy.	_____	_____

19. *"Design a logo" contest.* This one's for boosting morale and work unit spirit. An appropriate prize: Have a graphic artist render the logo, then frame a large and small version. Hang the large one in a public place and present the small one to the winning designer. For suggestions for things to do with the logo, see items 60 and 61 in Section 2.   _____   _____

ONGOING REWARD PROGRAMS

20. *Department recognition board.* Post citations, thank-you letters, customer commendations, and notes about each other. Solicit new items as necessary to keep the board full and the turnover frequent enough so that the board remains interesting.   _____   _____

21. *Frequent helper points.* Employees accumulate them by earning thank-you notes from coworkers (see item 94 in Section 3.) The person who garners so many thank-yous (you set the number) earns a prize.   _____   _____

22. *Frequent overtime points.* These are accumulated in the same way as frequent helper points, but are earned by working overtime. Both exempt and nonexempt employees should be eligible.   _____   _____

23. *"Service Ninja" Award.* This is used by Find/SVP, a research and consulting firm, to recognize the support people whose hard work isn't visible to clients. The sound of the theme song from *The Pink Panther* alerts everyone that a "Ninja" (dressed in costume) is about to appear with a surprise award. The unsuspecting recipient gets a Ninja sword, a cash award, and a personalized plaque. Each recipient's name goes on a large plaque hung in the hall. You can determine your own criteria for such an award, then seek out nominations by coworkers.   _____   _____

SECTION 2

SPONTANEOUS REWARDS

What's spontaneous about the rewards in this section is the decision to give one. Having them on hand to give may take some planning.

These are for those occasions when someone does something outstanding, often outside the person's regular job, that deserves special recognition. Or for the time when it suddenly dawns on you that an employee's (or a coworker's) steady contributions have gone relatively unheralded, and it's time to change that.

Many of these are token rewards. Their purpose is to remind the recipient of your appreciation and gratitude. So make sure you express those feelings clearly and specifically in conjunction with the reward. Otherwise, you risk giving the impression that the reward is a form of payment. The recipient's reaction to that is likely to be negative: "This company thinks that all my work is worth is a $10 T-shirt?" But when you put the reward in its proper context, the recipient will remember your appreciation each time he or she puts that T-shirt on.

When you select a reward for an individual, don't forget to consider that person's distinctive wants and needs. Remember to do unto the recipients as they would have you do unto them. The list below should give you choices to fit all tastes.

PRIVILEGES

Reward	Have Used	Will Use
24. *Do an employee's job for a day.* One day just before Christmas, visitors to a neighborhood bank in New York were surprised to find that the majority of tellers were middle-aged men. A discreet inquiry revealed that management had taken over the tellers' jobs for the day. You don't have to wait until Christmas.	_____	_____
25. *Morning coffee every day for a week hand-delivered by the manager.*	_____	_____
26. *Three-hour lunch break.* Great for holiday shopping but a nice surprise when spring flowers are in bloom too.	_____	_____
27. *Choice of late arrival or early leave-taking.* Especially appropriate as a reward for putting in long hours.	_____	_____
28. *A whole day off.*	_____	_____
29. *Casual dress day.* If your company has a regularly scheduled casual dress day, that doesn't count here. This is a special one to top off an exceptionally grueling effort by the entire team.	_____	_____
30. *Two hours of personal phone calls*—preferably not all at once.	_____	_____
31. *A work-at-home day.* Don't make a big deal of it. Rather, say something like, "Listen, if you'd be more comfortable finishing this up at home, go ahead. We'll cover the phone for you."	_____	_____
32. *Grab bag of privileges.* Print the ones listed above (and others you think of) on "gift certificates" and let the recipient draw or select one.	_____	_____

WORK ADJUSTMENTS

	Have Used	Will Use
33. *Increased authority.* Empower the employee to make monetary decisions, take actions without your signature, or supervise others.	_____	_____
34. *Designate the person as a project leader, with the opportunity to select other members of the team.*	_____	_____

Reward	Have Used	Will Use
35. *"Pick your project."* Allow the individual to determine the next assignment he will work on, within a predefined budget.	_____	_____
36. *"Do it your way."* A reward for the rebel in your group who always thinks there's a better way. Perhaps there is. Give this person a chance to try, backed up by reasonable resources.	_____	_____
37. *Swap a task.* Reward a coworker with an offer to trade for a day (or week) a task of yours she covets for one of hers she dislikes.	_____	_____
38. *A day to work on a favorite task only.* Arrange for coverage of the employee's other tasks so that this person doesn't return to a backlog the next day.	_____	_____
39. *"Pick a job for a day."* A day for the person to work at the job of his choice, along with or instead of the person who normally does it. Obviously, this needs the collaboration of everyone involved.	_____	_____
40. *Recognize a team accomplishment by designating that team a consultant to other teams.* Team members get the honor and others get the benefit of their skills. You may want to arrange for them to have some training in internal consulting skills.	_____	_____
41. *"How Can We Help?" Day.* This is a way for a whole team or work unit to show esteem for an overburdened and underrecognized coworker. Each person offers to assume one task for the person being recognized.	_____	_____

RECOGNITION THAT DOESN'T COST MONEY

42. *Write a letter to the employee's family,* expressing your appreciation for extra hours the employee has given to the job, and explaining specifically what he has done and what it means to you and the company.	_____	_____
43. *Set up a thank-you call from the president of the organization.*	_____	_____

Reward	Have Used	Will Use
44. *Arrange a visit from the president to acknowledge the contributions of an individual or your whole work unit.*	_____	_____
45. *Arrange to have an article in the organization's newsletter describing the accomplishments of an employee or team.*	_____	_____
46. *Write an "ad" for the newsletter,* touting your unit and the people who work in it and saying what it can do for other parts of the company.	_____	_____
47. *A thank-you letter signed by everyone in the work unit,* framed if you wish.	_____	_____
48. *"I stole _____'s idea and I'm using it" certificate.* Raychem Corporation created this idea to encourage people to capitalize on each other's work—to "steal" from each other.	_____	_____
49. *"I had an idea and _____ is using it" certificate.* A companion to item 48. This one goes to the person who came up with the idea in the first place.	_____	_____
50. *"World's Best . . ." certificate.* You can get software to produce an elegant one. Fill it in appropriately on the spur of the moment.	_____	_____
51. *Ring a bell and make an announcement when someone accomplishes a personal goal.*	_____	_____

AWARDS—"TROPHIES" AND GIFTS

	Have Used	Will Use
52. *Thank-you paperweight.* A note signed by you and the rest of the work unit, embedded in lucite.	_____	_____
53. *Establish and name an award after an employee.* If you create a Jane Doe Award for exceptional customer service, you honor Jane Doe again each time you present it to someone else. This suggestion comes from Caroline Meeks in *Small Business Reports,* December 1991.	_____	_____
54. *Donation to the employee's favorite charity in the employee's name.*	_____	_____

Reward	Have Used	Will Use
55. *Membership, in employee's name, in public television or radio.*	_____	_____
56. *Bottle of champagne sent to the employee's home.*	_____	_____
57. *Bouquet of flowers delivered to the office or home.* Don't save this for women only; men like flowers, too, and they seldom get them.	_____	_____
58. *Framed photograph of the employee with the organization president.*	_____	_____
59. *Gourmet gift.* Tailor it to the recipient's tastes: fancy coffee for a caffeine addict, expensive chocolate for a chocoholic, a basket of organic fruit for a health fanatic.	_____	_____
60. *T-shirts, hats, mugs with the department logo.* (Remember the contest in the previous section.)	_____	_____
61. *Silver or gold-plated pen with the company or department logo.* This is especially appropriate as recognition for an assignment involving heavy writing.	_____	_____
62. *Subscription to a professional magazine.*	_____	_____
63. *Book on a topic related to the recipient's work or future career plans.* Be sure to inscribe it with your thanks for a specific job well done.	_____	_____
64. *Lottery tickets.*	_____	_____
65. *Instant scratch-off cards.* Have them made up to reveal surprise gifts.	_____	_____
66. *Tickets to the theater or a sporting event.*	_____	_____
67. *Dinner for two at a restaurant of the recipient's choice.*	_____	_____
68. *Puzzle award for problem solvers.* Recognize someone who's solved a troublesome work problem with a metal ring or similar puzzle.	_____	_____
69. *Aiding and Abetting Plaque.* An award to recognize employees who freely give of their time, effort, and expertise to help others.	_____	_____
70. *Autographed picture of the recipient's favorite entertainment or sports personality.*	_____	_____

Reward	Have Used	Will Use
71. *New furniture or wall art.* Particularly impressive in a company where these require high-level approval.	_____	_____
72. *Framed cartoon related to the work done by the recipient.* Keep your eyes open and build up a collection of clipped cartoons that you can use for this purpose. This kind of reward says you care and that you really understand the person's job.	_____	_____
73. *Gift related to the recipient's hobby.* Call a family member or close friend to find out what the person really wants. Otherwise, it's easy to misjudge and get something that is too elementary, too sophisticated, or a duplicate of what the person already has.	_____	_____
74. *Gift certificate usable in a neighborhood specialty store related to the person's hobby.* This is a way to build community relations, too.	_____	_____
75. *T-shirts emblazoned with the employee's picture* (at work) *sent to members of the employee's family.*	_____	_____
76. *Gift certificate for lunch at a local restaurant for the recipient and a coworker.*	_____	_____
77. *The vault: a cabinet of various gift awards.* When you want to recognize someone on the spur of the moment, let that person choose. The ticket to the vault should be a letter or certificate that spells out the recipient's accomplishment.	_____	_____
78. *A selection of small gifts that any employee can present to any other employee to say "Thanks, you really helped me."* Accompany each gift with a certificate that the giver fills out, specifying the actions of the receiver that won recognition.	_____	_____
79. *A catalog of awards that recipients can choose from.*	_____	_____

EVENTS

	Have Used	Will Use
80. *Cook lunch for your group and bring it to the workplace.*	_____	_____

Reward	Have Used	Will Use
81. *Organize a car wash day, when all the managers wash employees' cars.* Who gets the car washes could be determined by a lottery.	_____	_____
82. *Breakfast for another work unit hosted by your group.* It could be bagels or a full buffet. Take it to a department that does a service for yours.	_____	_____
83. *Place an ad in a local newspaper, paying homage to your employees.* This is another idea from Meeks in *Small Business Reports*.	_____	_____
84. *Take an employee to lunch in the executive dining room.* If your organization doesn't have one, arrange an outside lunch in the company of a group of executives.	_____	_____
85. *Give a high-performing team a budget to host a party for another team.*	_____	_____
86. *"This Is Your Life."* Surprise an employee with a celebration recalling the highlights of her career. Bring in old friends, early managers, and executives.	_____	_____
87. *"This Is Your Life" scrapbook,* for someone who would be embarrassed by the attention if you held a celebration.	_____	_____
88. *Arrange for a team to present the results of its efforts to a group of upper-level management.*	_____	_____
89. *Create a photo collage of your employees at work and present it to your boss.* Make sure in advance that your boss will display it, and arrange for your people to see it displayed.	_____	_____

SECTION 3

DAY-TO-DAY FEEDBACK

No worker expects a bonus or a fancy award every day. But all workers have a right to expect day-to-day assurances that their work is on target, that their managers care about them, that the organization appreciates what they do.

This list contains things a manager can and should be doing every day to recognize employees for their contributions. And, since coworkers and bosses need feedback too, it includes a few vehicles for doing that. Most of them are very simple things we take for granted—and sometimes forget to do.

	Reward	Have Used	Will Use
90.	*"Thank you for _____,"* spoken aloud, publicly or privately. Be very specific.	_____	_____
91.	*"You did a good job on _____,"* Again, just say it, specifically.	_____	_____
92.	*A handwritten thank-you note to an employee,* with a copy in the recipient's personnel file.	_____	_____
93.	*A thank-you note to a coworker,* with a copy to the person's manager.	_____	_____
94.	*Thank-you sticky notes or notepads for everyone, to encourage their sending them to each other.*	_____	_____
95.	*"I couldn't have done it without you"* certificates, for everyone to give to anyone.	_____	_____
96.	*Small bulletin boards, designed to encourage people to "brag" a little by posting their*		

	Reward	Have Used	Will Use
	commendations or thank-you notes. Put a note from you on each board as you present it.	_____	_____
97.	*A handwritten thank-you note to your boss.*	_____	_____
98.	*A thank-you letter to an employee's family, thanking them for their sacrifices while the employee has been working extra overtime.*	_____	_____
99.	*An acknowledgement of an employee's or team's accomplishments broadcast widely via E-mail.*	_____	_____
100.	*An announcement of an employee's accomplishments to the person's customers, either external or internal.*	_____	_____

REVIEW

EXERCISE 14
SELF-ASSESSMENT AND ACTION PLAN

How often do you use the techniques covered in this book? Assessing your own behavior is a good way to pinpoint the areas in which you might want to do more toward recognizing and rewarding people in your organization. The items in the following list come from throughout the book. How often do you perform them?

A SELF-RATING CHECKLIST

Do You . . .	Never	Occa-sion-ally	Regu-larly
1. Make an effort to provide a total package of recognition and rewards that employees perceive as being equal to the value of their efforts?	____	____	____
2. Try to understand what needs drive your employees and to motivate them by providing rewards that meet those needs?	____	____	____
3. Remember to nurture high performers with positive feedback rather than taking them for granted?	____	____	____
4. Recognize small improvements in the behaviors and outputs of poor performers?	____	____	____

Do You . . .	Never	Occa-sion-ally	Regu-larly
5. Consistently reward behaviors that support the organization's stated values?	_____	_____	_____
6. Get input from employees regarding what rewards and reward criteria would best meet their needs?	_____	_____	_____
7. Ensure that all the people who report to you know what they must do to earn a reward?	_____	_____	_____
8. Track employees' progress and help them to overcome obstacles as they work toward accomplishing their goals?	_____	_____	_____
9. Offer primarily criteria-based rewards?	_____	_____	_____
10. Use competitions to generate excitement about a one-shot event rather than to spur ongoing performance improvement?	_____	_____	_____
11. Recognize behaviors as well as outcomes?	_____	_____	_____
12. Make an effort to reward people in a way *they* value rather than give rewards that appear valuable to you?	_____	_____	_____
13. Say "thank you" for routine work and incremental improvements?	_____	_____	_____
14. Tell your boss and peers "thank you" too?	_____	_____	_____
15. Make sure that you are very specific about the behaviors and outcomes you are praising when you give positive feedback?	_____	_____	_____
16. Enrich employees' jobs to make them interesting and challenging?	_____	_____	_____
17. Reward people for forming ad hoc teams to tackle problems?	_____	_____	_____

Do You . . .	Never	Occa- sion- ally	Regu- larly
18. Reward all team members equally for team accomplishments?	____	____	____
19. Reward cooperation rather than competition among employees?	____	____	____
20. Reward solving problems rather than covering them up?	____	____	____

ACTION PLANNING

Throughout this book you've been invited to make notes on the ways in which you'd like to improve your own methods of recognizing and rewarding people in your organization. Look back at those notes and at the items you marked "never" or only "occasionally" in the preceding checklist. From the information you've collected, identify three high-priority things you'd like to do right away to make better use of recognition and rewards to motivate people and to let them know how much you appreciate them.

Record those three action steps here.

1. _____
   _____
   _____

2. _____
   _____
   _____

3. _____
   _____
   _____

NOTES

NOTES

NOTES

NOTES

NOTES